POPCORN ROAD TO PARIS...
and Back

by Robert Wyatt Thrasher

Robert Wyatt Thrasher

authorHOUSE®

AuthorHouse™
1663 Liberty Drive, Suite 200
Bloomington, IN 47403
www.authorhouse.com
Phone: 1-800-839-8640

First published by AuthorHouse   10/23/2007

ISBN: 978-1-4343-1347-8 (sc)

Printed in the United States of America
Bloomington, Indiana

This book is printed on acid-free paper.

I dedicate this book to all soldiers and especially to the:

395th INFANTRY REGIMENT, 99TH DIVISION, COMPANY "L" – 3rd PLATOON

Lt. Colonel McClernand Butler

Pvt. Fred Ablin	Sgt Pyatt
Pfc Belcher	Pfc Regal
Pfc Biesboer	Pfc Runge
Sgt Billups	Lt. Sy Saffer
Pvt Bossham	Sgt Siemers
Pfc Billy Bradford	Pvt Skolba
Pfc Butler	Pfc Snodgrass
Sgt Cripes	Pfc Sopchak
Pfc Wayne Dean	Pfc Sykes
Pvt Duesenberry	Sgt Taylor
Pfc Finklea	Pvt. Theve
Pfc Fitzgerald	Pvt Toy
Pfc Furno	Pfc Tromble
Pvt Hartman	Pfc Vietti
Pfc Kuhn	Pfc Vizzini
Pfc Warren McCoy	Pfc Wadley
Sgt Mitchell	Sgt Wall
Pvt Mineheart	Pfc Walter
Sgt Murray	Pvt Irving Warnasch
Pfc Oxford	Pvt Wienstein
Sgt Olimpi	Pfc Wilkenson
Pfc Olson	Pfc Zarnfoller

Acknowledgment

I wish to thank everyone who has helped me. Without them, I could not have completed this project. I especially want to thank my daughters Nancy Sheehy and Carol Tolliver – for encouraging me to publish these stories, and for their assistance in typing and editing. I also want to thank my wife, Bessie, and my other daughters, Linda Harper, Jane Canter, Susan Parker and my son, Robert W. Thrasher, Jr. for being my audience over the years. I also want to thank Joan Hershey and Dale Enochs for their encouragement

TABLE OF CONTENTS

FOREWORD

This book contains a collection of "memories" from my experiences during World War II as well as some short stories about my childhood. Several of my stories are about the army buddies I shared foxholes with and who stood with me as we fought the Germans. Some of them were killed right in front of me. I don't know how I managed to escape being wounded while others who were only inches away were killed. I suspect I had a guardian angel to protect me, and I was meant to write about them and forever preserve their memories.

I served as a scout in the 99th Division, 395th Infantry, Company L. I received basic training at age 18 in Arkansas, then I was sent to the Army Specialized Training Program (ASTP) at the University of Arkansas, and later I was stationed at Camp Maxey in Paris, Texas. After training, Company L was shipped to England and then to France.

I fought in the Battle of the Bulge and also saw action at Bergheim, Remagen, the Ruhr Pocket and Gleidorf. Later our battalion joined the Third Army which was commanded by General Patton. I received numerous medals including a Bronze Star, A Presidential Unit Citation, an Expert Infantry Badge, a Combat Infantry Badge, and a Belgian Fourragere.

After Hitler was defeated, I anticipated being shipped immediately to fight the Japanese. Figuring I would never get to see Paris otherwise, I decided to go AWOL and visit the city. Later when I reported to my commander, he gave me a choice: I could be court-martialed, or I could "ship out." I chose to "ship out." Not knowing the destination, several others and I were loaded onto a truck bound for our new assignment. Imagine my reaction when I found myself back in Paris. The Army was nice enough to put me up in a hotel for approximately the next six months, and I was given a tough job. What I had to do was to oversee the delivery of supplies to the numerous Army headquarters in Paris. During this time, I met a Parisian girl who helped me with my French. Her family embraced me, and I visited their home enjoying many meals with them.

The sad day arrived when the Army shipped me back home to Harrodsburg, Indiana in 1946. I had been away for almost three years.

I returned to live with my parents as my help was needed on the farm. I soon met my future wife Bessie Nilson, and we were married in 1947.

I dedicate this book to the men who served with me in the 3rd Platoon, L Company. Their names appear at the beginning of this book.

Following is a letter written by the author to his mother and father.

Elfershausen, Germany , Fri. May 25,1945
Dear Folks:

Received two letters from you today and one from JoAnn. Am very happy to hear that you finally heard that I'm O.K. I know how you felt and I wouldn't have had it happen for anything. You wanted to know the particulars so here is the gist of it. I got lost on the nite of Apr. 24 in the neighborhood of the Beautiful Blue Danube River--which isn't so beautiful and isn't so blue. That nite the company pushed ahead and when I tried to catch up I took the wrong road and wound up in a little German town. I was the only G.I. in town. By the time I had gotten out of there and caught up with the company about five days had passed, so naturally they thought I was missing.

They've stopped censorship now so I can tell some things I couldn't before. The town I'm in is close to Frankfort and we are in the 3rd Army now and have been since the 1st of April. After we crossed the Rhine, we were one of the first three outfits across, we fought our way out of the bridgehead area, then helped in the encirclement of the Ruhr. We fought in the Ruhr pocket and in one afternoon our "Bn." (Battalion) took 5,000 German prisoners but it was some of the worst fighting we'd seen. After the Ruhr pocket our Div. went to the 3rd Army and we drove almost to Czechoslovakia, then turned south toward the Danube, crossed it and were within a few miles of Munich when the war ended. I was really sweating out those last few days as was everyone. I know how you must have felt to have heard I was missing one day after the war was over.

We don't know yet if we are going to Pacific or are going to be Occupation, but in either case it's doubtful if I'll get to come home. I can speak German pretty fair now. I can say almost anything I want to although it's not grammatically correct, naturally. I've got 48 points which isn't good, but it's about average or better I imagine.

I'll start a history of our experiences if you want to hear it, beginning in Texas. I don't remember the dates so I'll just guess at them and all casualties etc. All I'll mention will just be men from our platoon. There are forty men in a platoon. This will be just a digest. I may enlarge on it and may not. All of us boys have agreed on why soldiers don't usually tell civilians of their experiences, they won't believe them. But here goes anyhow and I'll leave out the more incredible parts. We left Maxey about 15th of Sept. 1944 and went to Camp Miles Standish, Mass. About 10 miles from Boston. On Sept. 29 we went aboard ship "The Marine Devil" and sailed in a huge convoy to Plymouth, England. There were over 75 ships with us, including aircraft carriers and destroyers.

We also had dirigibles with us the first two days out. We had one submarine alert but no ships were sunk. On Oct. 10 we landed and went to Marabout Barracks in Dorchester, England. We stayed there three weeks training like the devil. Then we left by train for Southampton, England and sailed for LeHarve, France. We were in France only two days, in Belgium four, then on Nov. 10 we went on line at Hofen, Germany, right in the middle of the Siegfreid Line where we remained for three months; with deep snow on the ground every day. I don't think the sun shined more than five times while we were there. Our job was to defend the town which sat on a high hill. I've already told you quite a bit about what happened there. We butchered cows, chickens, and hogs and ate pretty well, but we were running patrols almost every nite, and were under German artillery and mortar 24 hrs. a day.

On Nov. 24, Thanks. Eve, we ran a patrol out into no mans land and had just crossed a creek and were walking up an old wagon road with Sgt. Murray and I in the lead. (It was about 10 o'clock at nite) when they opened up on us and Sgt. Murray was killed. It was my first close experience with death and I took it much better than I thought I would. Then a few weeks later we were running a similar patrol when two of our boys stepped on a mine. One Pfc. Oxford was killed and Pfc. Butler lost an arm and leg. He's in a hospital in Utah now and he writes us pretty often. He's taking it O.K.

Then a little later we were building a road block and our new squad leader Sgt. Mitchell got a piece of mortar shrapnel in his leg, breaking it all to pieces. He's in the states too and is doing O.K. Then came Von

Rundstedts offensive, he threw an entire div. at our battalion, 10,000 men against 900. But although Hofen was surrounded it never fell, the casualties, all only slightly wounded. I was in the hospital for ten days along there somewhere and came back New Years Eve. At that time our platoon were in foxholes continually out in front of town. The snow was about two feet deep and it snowed almost everyday.

The first nite I was back, Pfc. Fitzgerald was killed by a booby trap. At midnite the Heinies celebrated by opening up on us with everything they had. They were in nice, warm pillboxes, we were too cold to celebrate. It was along in here sometime a Kraut Patrol walked over the top of my fox hole. That was a close one. I was also first scout on a combat patrol along in Jan., 2 men were killed and 3 wounded but they weren't from our platoon. Then in a little attack in the middle of Jan., Sgt. Taylor and Olson were killed by mines and Pvt. Dusenberry wounded. Then in the latter part of Jan. We were relieved for three days then we went on line again at the bottom of a huge hill near Schleiden, Germany. We were there only a week when we left to go back to Belgium for about 20 days of rest. We had several boys evacuated for combat fatigue and trench foot by this time, too.

After leaving Belgium we went on the attack again, we crossed the Roer River at the much publicized city of Duren. It was the most completely destroyed large city I have ever seen. There was nothing standing, not a wall or tree; Aachen was in good shape compared to it. Our battalion was the first to cross the Erft River, which was holding up the entire First Army. We crossed it at about 2:00 A.M. and entered the town of Bergherim (about 20000 pop.) on the other side. We fought in it all day and by nite were just on the other side of town. The Engineers had a bridge in by that time and the next day the 3rd Armored Div. Pushed thru us, but we went along and helped them take the next town, then they took off and drove clear to Cologne.

Our platoon had no casualties then tho the rest of the company didn't fare so well. It's a wonder we didn't tho, as we were both bombed and strafed, shelled by artillery and rockets, sniped at and machine gunned and had direct fire from Heinie tanks. It first seemed tho that as soon as we left one spot the Krauts would just blow it up with artillery, so we were always one jump ahead of them that time. The next day we angled off north of Cologne and drove clear to the Rhine just opposite from Dusseldorf. We didn't do it in one day tho. It took us about five, walking all the time. We were lucky on casualties again. Sgt. Cripes was wounded in the leg when we were ambushed just outside of one town and Pvt. Minehart was seriously wounded in the arm just when we had reached the Rhine.

We took a hell of a lot of prisoners tho and killed quite a few. We stayed there looking at Dusseldorf several days. We were afraid we might have to cross the Rhine then and take the town. Nights the Air Corps would bomb it and search lights would go on and the sirens wail and the Heinies would throw artillery at us so we couldn't enjoy the show. The Air Corps does a good job, their dive bombers worked with us all the time, helping take towns and knocking our tanks and artillery that was giving us trouble. But everybody knows they are good, they are paid like it and treated like it. We know we are good too.

Then the 1st Army took the Bridge at Remagen, that nite we took off down the bank of the Rhine and crossed the bridge next afternoon. The Heinies were shelling and bombing it all the time but we were lucky and no one was hit, although a lot of guys laying there in the road and ditches weren't so lucky. The Hienies were using big stuff and the guys who were hit were hardly ever left in less than three or four pieces.

I don't know what the papers said, but in one little wheat field across the bridge I seen no less than 500 dead Germans and Americans, Germans outnumbering the Americans about three to one. Just from the position of the bodies you could see how the battle went. A company of Americans were attacking across the field when a larger force of Heinies counter attacked and surrounded them. The Heinies were then in a position to threaten the bridge, so all the artillery we had in the area opened up on that little field and wiped out everyone-- what's a couple hundred lives compared to a bridge.

We have been in the same position a few times ourselves, but some of us made it through it O.K. In fact we were in the same position a nite later. We attacked in the morning and had advanced to an old quarry, but we were stopped there by tanks and machine guns. We had several men killed and wounded during the day, but that nite was the topper.

We were afraid the Heinies would counter attack that nite, so just after dark we were going to withdraw and let all of our artillery give the place we just left hell in case the Heinies followed us. But the artillery got ahead of itself for some unknown reason (there was a bit stink about it, naturally) and fifteen battalions (240 guns) shelled us for ten minutes before we could get it stopped. What was left of the company then retreated as planned. The Comp. Commander was so mad he cried. We rested for a week then till we could get in replacements. Miraculously no one in the third platoon was hit, altho several went back from combat fatigue.

The third platoon has had the fewest casualties by far in the company. Besides the artillery which came so close it knocked me off the ground several times I had another narrow escape that afternoon. The second scout and I walked right up on two German machine guns and both opened up on us at 75 yds. range while we were out in the open. We ran back about 15yds. to a pile of rocks and the bullets were kicking up dirt all around us just like in the movies. I was so sure I'd been hit I stuck my hand under my clothes to feel for blood. Some guys in similar circumstances have been so sure they were hit that they took their wound tablets.

It was during this week of rest I went back to get my tooth pulled and Lloyd was looking for me. I had to go clear back across the Rhine to get it done. After the replacements came in we went on attack again about 11p.m. one night. Our Bn (battalion) spearheaded an attack across the Rhine River. It was rumored we were going to get another Presidential citation for that, but I guess it was only a rumor.

All that night, the next day and next night we fought through the German lines around the bridgehead. The last night we went up so far so fast we captured a Heinie regiment C.P. intact, colonel and all. By morning, we had broken through their lines completely and we got on tanks and encircled the Ruhr. But during the break three of my good friends in the platoon were killed. Pfc. Virgil Wadley of Oklahoma was hit square in the chest by four machine gun bullets and died immediately. Pfc Belcher was hit in the shoulder by the same machine gun.

Some of the new replacements were hit too, but I don't remember their names nor how many. There's nothing more pitiful than a new replacement. He comes with a hopeful look in his eye, but we can't return it. He has clean, new clothes and equipment, is clean-shaven and wondering what the hell is going to happen next. But he's better off than we are in one way, he doesn't know what to be afraid of, but we do. We even have to tell some of them to get down when the Heinies start shooting at us.

We didn't have much trouble in the encirclement of the Ruhr. We just went through towns collecting prisoners and searching houses, we hardly had to fire a shot. But when we got to the end of the pocket and started working back toward the Rhine everything got rougher including the weather. When we go on the attack, we don't carry any blankets or overcoat, only a raincoat.

We were up in some pretty high hills then and it started snowing, and got colder than the dickens. When it quit snowing, it started raining. For four straight days and nights we lived in it before we took a town and could get a hold of a civilian blanket. It got so bad we bitched like hell if some other company got to take a town instead of us. If they had some trouble and were quite a while taking it we'd want to go in and show them how to do it in a hurry. Usually when we took a town we'd stay in it a day or so and rest up.

But to get back to the subject. We attacked down a valley one morning about 4:00 a.m. and had gone about 1,000 yards when we hit heavy machine gun and tank fire. Our own tank fired on us too to top it off. One boy was hit in the arm about three feet away from me with a bullet. We maneuvered around and the tanks with us did too but we seemed to get in a little deeper every time we moved. Guys were getting hit left and right. We lost about thirty. The captain was hit that afternoon. We had one killed and several wounded in the Third Platoon that day, but I don't remember their names.

Our tanks weren't much help that day, besides firing into us they took off and left us when a Heinie tank opened up on them and knocked one out. In fact we all have a poor opinion of our tanks. They have failed us so much. But when there is no opposition the tanks look nice rolling down a road. Just before dark we retreated because we couldn't advance any more and guys were getting hit all the time.

The outfit over in the next valley didn't have so much trouble on top of a hill behind them. They had just taken a huge hill in front of us but the Germans counter attacked and while we were digging in the Germans run them off. It took them four hours to do it and there was so much small arms fire it looked like the woods were burning from the smoke. And for the past two days it had rained and it was so foggy now you could hardly see and it was that way all day the next day. It was pretty cold too and we were wet all the time. We were in real thick pine forests all the time. I'd rather fight in towns any day than forests. At night it's so dark you can't see anything and it's hard to dig in from the roots. The artillery is worse too as it goes off in the tree tops and all the shrapnel comes right down on your back.

Now, back to my story. We were dug in right at the edge of a steep hill overlooking a little town which the Heinies were in. They had a tank down there too and it's 88 was pointing right up the hill at us. Our artillery pounded the town all night and the woods around it, but it didn't stop us from sleeping, wet as we were. We stood guard one hour and then slept one hour all night every night so you see we hardly got any beauty rest.

I almost got shot by one of the replacements. He was in the foxhole with me and was nervous as the dickens. I stood guard outside the foxhole and when I got back in to wake him up he humped up and pointed his rifle at me, then I hollered at him. He left a day later for combat fatigue. (Just got three letters from you written 15, 11, and 12th of April. You needn't tell Mrs. Clark so but her son is more than likely either killed or wounded as "F" Co. was almost completely wiped out when we crossed the Danube).

The next morning the outfit in front of us retook their hill and we followed them up, they then went straight on and we turned off towards a town a couple miles off. It was raining like the dickens and foggy. At times like that your morale is very low. We advanced to within less than a half mile of the town by nite having running fights with the Germans all the way. They kept shooting at us and then running back a little way. We dug in that nite at the edge of a woods close to a highway going into town. In the meantime the rest of the Battalion came into the other side of town and after quite a bit of fighting took it just a little after dark.

We could see Heinie tanks and vehicles going up and down the road in front of us, but they didn't know exactly where we were and never did get the range on us. During the night the Heinies counter-attacked the town with one tank in support and retook 3/4's of it. They also captured quite a few of our boys. The one Heinie tank knocked out three of ours, and really raised hell. So the next morning our company left the woods and ran across the open field into town and took it in about four hours.

Town fighting is really hard work as the Heinies lock every door on every house and you have to run across the yards between houses with the Heinies shooting at you and then either shoot or beat the door down with them still shooting at you. It's really hard work. You are pretty well pooped after 2 or 3 hours of running, jumping, and beating down doors. Our platoon had two wounded in the town, Pfc. Dean and a replacement, but the company had four killed and several wounded. That was the last time one of the regular platoon boys was seriously hurt. We had a few more wounded and the company had several killed and wounded afterwards, but for the third platoon the casualties were about over.

You have heard about streets running with blood, well it was almost that way in this town, because it had changed hands three times and there were dead and wounded Heinies everywhere, big pools of blood in nearly every house and in the streets. It stinks from it, almost made me sick. We took a few prisoners, another boy and I took about fifteen. For once the tanks helped us out like they were made to do.

We went down the street in both rows of buildings and the tank went right down the middle of the street with us, blasting at the houses just in front of us. It was pretty easy running them out of town that way. But once they were out of town the fight wasn't over.

The town sat right at the bottom of three hills and the Heinies ran up in the woods and sniped and machined gunned us every time we'd stick our nose out. Guys were getting hit pretty often too. But we stayed there the rest of the day and that night and real early the next morning we took off toward the hills around town without too much trouble, then it was just taking more towns and more hills for the next three days.

Our platoon was very lucky and didn't have any casualties during this time if I remember right, although I can't say the same for the rest of the Company. At that time we had about broken thru the Heinies defenses and had them going around in circles, so we piled on tanks and high-balled it down the main roads, overtaking and shooting up Heinie convoys, most of them horses and wagons. It was hell on the horses, as a lot of them got hurt and killed. It was hell on the men too. We left them laying dead and wounded in both ditches, and the prisoners were going back down the road by the thousands, our battalion alone took over five thousand that day.

That night at dark we came to a big town that was just full of German prisoners. We were a little worried as the Germans were running around everywhere. We really got a lot of loot there, that's when I got my pistols. Then the next day we walked quite a ways to the next town and took part of it before dark, but the prisoners told us there were 27,000 allied POW'S in the town, so we called a truce and finally the Heinies agreed to call it an open city. So they moved out and we moved in to take care of the prisoners.

All these prisoners, mostly Russians, were just in a small field, and one artillery shell would have killed hundreds. They were practically starved and some were insane, so we had to keep them in or they would have raised hell. I remember a dog got in there somehow and they grabbed it, tore it to pieces and ate it raw. We caught some who had got out, dug up a dead horse and were eating it. One had the tail gnawing on it with the hair still on. When we came they were dying at the rate of two hundred a day and the Germans were burying them all in one grave. It was two days before we could feed them as we had outrun our supply lines.

After about three days we left there, joined Patton's Army and drove towards Czechoslovakia, then we turned south, crossed the Danube, and at the end of the war were just a little east of Munich. I could enlarge on this, but I'm getting tired of writing. So had better quit. Will write more later.

Love,
Robert

You wanted to know how many battle stars I have--three (Ardennes, East and West of the Rhine), Just counted and we have fourteen men now out of the original forty who left Camp Maxey and five of the fourteen have been wounded and came back. The only wound I've got so far in this war is a cut on my right thumb from opening a can of C Rations.

My First Job

IN THE EARLY FORTIES jobs were hard to find. Then came Hitler, and defense jobs opened up -- but not for young boys -- they knew the boys would be in the Army soon, so boys couldn't get a real job. I lived on a farm, worked mainly at home and for other farmers. Sometimes I worked in a saw mill. None of them paid anything and I never had any money.

Then I was in the Army. I got a dollar a day -- $30 a month with room and board. I never had so much money, even after paying for my insurance. We boys wanted our mothers to get some money if we were killed, so we had a little over $7 a month taken out of our pay. Now people sue about everything, but no lawyer has ever offered to get any $7 a month back.

I didn't know what to do with all that money. I'd eat a whole pint of ice cream by myself – it was only 15 cents, I think. And Army work was easier than working in a saw mill -- off-bearing green sycamore cross ties. All we did was learn to march in step, how to shoot a rifle, do the manual of arms, salute, live outdoors in a little tent, and hike a lot carrying everything with you. Then I went to Europe as a first scout in the Infantry. I still did the same things, only with somebody trying to kill me both night and day.

To show their appreciation, the Army gave me a Combat Infantry Badge and a $10 a month raise. I was in real money now and sent most of it home to my mother who bought war bonds with it. When I got home I cashed the bonds and bought an old Chevy with over 100,000 miles on it. Money well spent. I never got killed so my mother never got any money.

I soon got used to my job as a scout. I learned to concentrate really hard and be aware of everything all the time. I can tell you that it was a kid's job. An old man sure couldn't handle it. But before you knew it, the war was over and I was laid off. That damn Hitler again.

I've had a lot of jobs since then, and I don't remember much about any of them. But I sure do remember that first one.

THE DESERVING

AT THE TIME IT WAS SOMETHING you didn't want to think about. Or if you did you wanted to blame the victim. I'm talking about the deaths of your fellow soldiers. You needed to think they had somehow deserved it. They didn't try hard enough. They did stupid things. They didn't listen when you told them what to do. They deserved it.

You needed to believe that. Since you weren't that stupid and tried harder, you weren't going to die. I've never yet thought this through. I'm just writing what pops into my head. I'm probably not trying hard enough and am just being stupid. But now and then someone died who tried harder than you did and was smarter than you and you knew didn't deserve to die. What then? Was everything just fate? If so, what was the use of trying so hard?

Sometimes you were in a position when you knew you were going to die. There was no way out. This was it. But you didn't die. This happened over and over and you didn't die. There was only one answer. You were God's chosen.

I'm not sure I remember the spelling, but German soldiers had belt buckles with "Gott mit uns" on them. It meant, "God is with us." An old joke says Germans would yell at Americans, "Gott mit uns." The smart aleck Americans would yell back, "We got mittens too." Everybody thought they were God's chosen.

You developed an unhealthy attitude where you didn't respect death. It was everywhere. Babies, children, women, and old men. They were just landfill material and sometimes that's what you did with the bodies. Dig a trench with a bulldozer and shove the bodies in and cover them up. I don't think you get over that. I don't know, but I think it taints the rest of your life.

I think I do have a solution to all these problems—Most people who are screaming about going somewhere and making war on someone know they or theirs won't have to go, or if they do, they will be in a safe position and they can yell and threaten and feel good about themselves.

We need a U.N. resolution or something that says all combat soldiers in the future will be over forty-five years of age. Everyone goes, man or woman, rich or poor, black or white. No exceptions, and no exemptions. That's it. You go.

You say you have a heart condition and your wife is in ill health. So what. You can still stop a bullet, can't you? Let the teenagers stay home and get rich making munitions. I don't know much, but I do know that would be the end of war for all time on this planet.

And death. It's out there. In the dark. Waiting. If you don't try hard enough, or are just stupid, or don't pay attention, it'll get you. Sure as Hell.

CAMPIN' OUT

I'M OLD NOW, KIND OF LIKE an old dog that lies in front of the fire, dreaming about chasing rabbits and things, barking and jerking in his sleep. But once I was young and full of piss and vinegar, looking for travel and adventure.

And I got lucky; when I was eighteen in 1943, an organization offered me a chance to back pack Europe, all expenses paid, and even pay me a little while I did it. Who the hell could turn that down? Of course, as I found out later, there was a catch or two. But isn't there, always.

Anyway, I signed up for the trip. I then spent several months in various swamps and deserts in the US, learning how to camp out. Whenever we were going to camp it was always at least 25 miles away, and we had to walk there in the heat of the day, with little or no water, carrying all kinds of useless crap. When we got to the camp ground, it was always dark; but the first thing we had to do was dig a great big hole. In case we died during the night, we'd have our grave dug, I guess.

But there were compensations, one of which was called short arm inspection. This was done to see if you had venereal disease. They told us you got this by consorting with low-type women – whatever the hell that is. Hell, we never saw any women, low life or high. The nearest we got to sex was being screwed by the people in charge of the damned outfit.

But anyway, we had lots of short arm inspections. And like everything else we did, we had a lot of dry runs. A dry run is practicing something you are going to do without really doing it. Whenever we had a short arm inspection, we were told to line up in the street with

5

nothing on but shoes, socks, raincoats, and helmet liners. A guy would come along and stop in front of you and say, "Skin it back and milk it down." I'm glad to say they acted like they enjoyed their work. But then, so did we. Most things in life work out for the best, I've always found. God, I still miss those short-arm inspections.

And you had to learn how to pitch a little bitty tent for just two people. I was always paired off with some damned pervert. I'd wake up in the middle of the night with some jackass holding me in his arms, slobbering on my neck, and a big hard on against my tender ass. He'd always claim he was asleep and dreaming. Sure. I'm slow, but I did learn to use that excuse myself. It still works, I'm glad to say. Male or female, they buy it. About the same percentage even, whatever that proves.

You also had to learn how to wash dishes, pans, floors, walls, ceilings; and as the saying goes, anything that doesn't move. I learned to wash refrigerators. I discovered that the people in charge kept all the good stuff to eat in there while they fed us the things that had either spoiled or were on the verge of spoiling. The people in charge liked my initiative and imagination. They never learned that all I did was eat all I could hold and steal off their good stuff. This is a good thing to remember.

Then you had to learn to walk in unison with a big group of people; to move almost like a big flock of black birds in a field. The people in charge would watch to see that we were in perfect alignment. We learned little tricks to mess them up. Such as taking turns bobbing our heads up when everyone else was bobbing theirs down. The people in charge really got pissed off about that. But you do what you can.

Then you had to learn to hold your breath in a room full of poison gas, while getting your gas mask out and putting it on. This was a snap for me. I used to sleep in a bed full of little boys during the Depression when all you had to eat was beans. Those little shits could let farts that would set your eyebrows on fire. I learned to hold my breath for hours. You couldn't survive any other way. Thank God we don't live in a world like that any more.

The biggest thing we had to learn was to revere and respect our betters. That was hard for me to do, even to this day. Being dumb, I always asked myself why was he my better. I still don't know the answer. Maybe in another world. But like a lot of things, you soon could fake it. It worked. Still does.

The enforcement of discipline was another matter. One kid dropped a cigarette butt on the ground. His penalty was, after a full day of physical training, to dig a six by six by six foot hole in the ground and bury the offending butt in it. Afterwards, he apparently wasn't happy enough about the whole thing, and had the privilege of digging it up again. I don't remember if he kicked the habit or not. I hope so.

Saluting your betters was another great privilege we enjoyed. You could usually avoid the process if you did it just right. But it was dangerous. My best General George Patton story is about failing to salute, and the result of the failure. We were somewhere in central Germany in March of '45. We had been around a lot of prison and death camps of all descriptions. The inmates of these camps had every disease and parasite known to man. They naturally gave some of it to us. Scratching your cooties was about the only thing we could that gave us pleasure. Of course something had to be done about that. One muddy day in the middle of a gigantic sleet storm, we had to go through a delousing station. After standing for hours in freezing slush, icicles hanging from our noses, waiting to be deloused, we saw Gen. Patton approaching at maximum speed, throwing slush both ahead and behind. Nobody said anything, but we just all turned our backs.

Patton's vehicle zoomed by with him screaming at his driver to halt and back up. The driver did so, throwing more freezing slush all over us. Patton then stood up in the back of the vehicle, turned purple, and proceeded to address us at great length. The gist of it was that we were the scum of the earth; the illegitimate progeny of diseased, demented, perverted creeps. And if we ever turned our back on him again, the best we could hope for was to die and go to Hell quickly. The next time I saw him he was doing the same thing to officers. The second time was a lot more fun. For me, at least.

Of course we had to learn other things in training. One was bayonet drill. I'm sorry I can't remember anything funny about that. Not to this day.

But something funny did happen learning to get through barbed wire entanglements. We had a great sergeant. Sgt. Murray. He had a great sense of humor, and was a born leader. After Sgt. Murray showing and explaining to us how to get through the wire the proper way, one smart ass kid said, "Why not do it this way."

He then took off running at the wire, attempting to jump over it. He caught his foot in the wire and dived right through the whole mess. It tore all his clothes off and scratched and bloodied him up somewhat. Sgt. Murray approached him lying there, all bloody and helpless; saw that he would survive, and said only, "That's why." We loved it.

While I'm talking about Sgt. Murray, I might as well finish the story. There is something to be learned about it, but I don't like the answer. Life is not fair and God doesn't necessarily favor the best and brightest.

On the ship going to Europe, Sgt. Murray was very sea sick. He was so sick he said he wanted to die. On getting on land again, Sgt. Murray said, "Unless they build a bridge, I'm not going home, I'll stay right here." They didn't build a bridge and he did stay there. He's still there fifty-two years later, as I write this. He was the first guy killed in our little group. He was killed standing at my elbow on our first patrol. Why him and not me, I don't know. The same thing happened many more times. Too many. Why them and not me. I don't know.

When we finally returned from our patrol in the early hours of the following day, we didn't know what to do. He was the first guy killed and we loved him very much. He was also the best soldier of us all. How could that happen? It really bothered us. But we solved the problem.

We were issued emergency rations periodically which we were supposed to save and eat only when we had nothing else. The ration was a form of hard, concentrated chocolate candy. We always ate ours as quick as we got them.

But, being a good soldier, Sgt. Murray saved his. His ammo bag was full of them. After an hour or two of not knowing how to handle his death, someone – I hope it was me – said the right thing, "Let's divide up his chocolate." It was the right thing to say. It worked. Sgt. Murray would have approved. He'd spent a lot of time and effort teaching us how to solve problems, and we had just solved our first one without him.

My God. Come Look.
They're Eating White Bread

My God. Come look. They're eating white bread.

I remember that because I thought it was so stupid. I know now that I was the one that was stupid for not understanding what they meant.

It was about noon on a warm March day in central Germany. We had just finished taking a town that had given us a little trouble. It was shot up quite a bit and had lots of dead bodies lying around.

Our rarely seen kitchen crew brought us noon chow. For reasons I will explain I remember exactly what it was. Pork and beans and a big slab of white bread. My buddy and I were sitting on the curb eating our pork and beans when he pointed out that they looked exactly like a German soldier's brains that were lying in the street in front of us.

We kept on eating. That sounds impossible now but I think it shows that you can get used to anything. We noticed the civilians were beginning to look out of the cellars. We ignored them. We had taken a town yesterday and we would take another one tomorrow. That's what we did.

But it was the civilians' first experience with something like this. Since we ignored them, the civilians got braver and started walking up the street toward us. It seemed they were only interested in us. They were ignoring their torn up town and the dead bodies.

One young woman, holding a child by the hand, was braver than the rest and came up very close to my buddy and me. She was close enough to see what we were eating. Suddenly she turned and yelled to the others. We knew enough German to know what she was saying.

"My God. Come look. They're eating white bread."

9

So stupid. Her nation destroyed, her town destroyed the young men about all dead. Years of deprivation, rationing, shortages behind them and years more ahead of them while they rebuilt. And all they were interested in was that we were eating white bread.

I know now that she was the most optimistic person I'd ever met. She meant that the war was over for her and her child. It looked like they would live. It was spring and the sun was shining.

And maybe she wasn't, but other people in the world were even eating white bread again.

LOST AND FOUND

———⇒>●<⇐———

I KEEP HAVING SIXTY-ONE YEAR OLD memories in detail. I can't even remember what I had for breakfast, or if I even had breakfast. So I usually eat again to make sure. An infantry soldier at the front had very few possessions and couldn't afford to lose any of them because the only way to replace it was to steal it or take it off of a dead soldier.

If you were in open country like the northern Rhineland, there was no place to hide, especially from tanks. A soldier stood out in that flat, open country like a bowling pin and believe me, tanks really liked to knock down spares.

So you really loved your entrenching tool which was an adjustable, combination pick and shovel which you carried in a little pouch on your ammo belt. You carried eight clips of rifle shells, your first-aid kit, your canteen, your bayonet, and your entrenching tool on your ammo belt. Your beloved helmet, which was a combination hiding place if you had nothing else, served as a cooking pot, a wash basin, and sometimes a chamber pot (you did try to wash it out sometimes if you could). You wore it on your head at all times. You slept in it and always kept it on except, of course, when you had to defecate in it.

Other possessions you carried in your little back pack and your ammo bag, which was a small bag on a strap across your shoulder. I kept my prize possessions in my ammo bag – cigarettes, k-rations, emergency candy bars, and a little ammo.

One day a tank caught me in the middle of an open field and was sending machine gun tracers flying by my head. I went flying back for some woods to hide in. When I was completely exhausted from running and zigzagging, I would hit the ground for a short rest, and every time my ammo bag was in front of my crotch and made my ass

11

stick up in the air at least six inches. But it felt like it was up a flag pole, so I threw my ammo bag away with all my prize possessions.

One day I lost my entrenching tool. I nearly went nuts. When you are on defense, you dig a little hole to get away from the bullets. It's literally the difference between life and death. I had to have another one and the only way to get one was find a dead American and take his. But that day I couldn't find one. We were in front of everyone and all the dead guys were behind us.

Finally, just before dark, to my great relief I found a dead GI, and got his shovel. He gave his life for his country and a shovel for me. About dark we were attacked near a big old building with a wall around it. I dug a foxhole behind the wall and felt safe again. We investigated the building. It was a convent or nunnery and the basement was an emergency hospital and in it were wounded Germans and a few Americans.

No, I've never been happy to find a dead American since then. I guess you would have had to been wearing my shoes.

My Day With the Colonel

It was probably early March and we were just a few miles from the Rhine River. It was a great spring day and we were not meeting any resistance from the Germans, which always made the day better. We had some tanks with us, but I don't remember which division they were from. The little town we were going through had bed sheets hanging out the windows. That meant they surrendered, and not to shoot it up.

I was first scout and when I left this town, I was joined by Col. Butler and his radio man. Col. Butler was the battalion commander and as a scout I had never been joined by anyone before, let alone a colonel. The Colonel had his map case and he told me we were just a few kilometers from the Rhine and we would reach it that day. I think he was probably trying to speed me up a little, as there was a chance we would be the first outfit to reach the river, and that would be a big honor.

I know I wasn't paying much attention until a bunch of fireflies flew past my head and I knew we were in bad trouble. We retreated back to the first house and the Colonel called in artillery on his radio.

We had self-propelled artillery from the Armored Division just behind us. It was very good and literally blew the Germans out of the ground. But we didn't leave this town until just before daylight the next morning. I was first scout again. We ran into Germans about noon and didn't reach the Rhine until the next day. I can remember running down to the water, but thought someone was looking at me from the bank and ran back. From there we went to Remagen and more fun.

I didn't spend any time with colonels again, and if that's how they spend their time I don't want to.

HEADQUARTERS

I've just finished my tax forms and am waiting on the veterinary to doctor a sick calf. The news has had a lot about Wall Street millionaires defrauding people of billions of dollars and only getting a slap on the wrist or sometimes a kiss on the cheek. If they had robbed a 7-11 Store of fifty dollars, they would have been sentenced to years in the pen, and life if they did it again. And this is the world's greatest democracy!

Because of Iraq, I think a lot about military service and the democracy of that. It's a well- kept secret, but it was government policy in WWII to put poor, uneducated rural and southern white boys in the infantry. And they were used like tissues--throw them away and get another boy; they don't cost anything. The vast majority of casualties were teen-age riflemen in the infantry.

I think the public, the news, and other soldiers had to look down on the infantry to keep feeling superior. The place to be in was Headquarters. Ah...they knew everything. Did everything. Even won the war. I was just a dumbass rifleman in the infantry until one day the 9th Infantry Division was attacking through my division, the 99th, and I was loaned out to a Headquarters unit in the 9th Division. I think it was in Monschau, just inside Germany. I was a first scout in a rifle platoon and had been on a lot of patrols in the area. They told me that since I knew the area so well, they loaned me out in case the other division had problems.

I was taken to their Headquarters in a jeep and they were in a nice building with a hot fire in the stove. I never did anything but sat in the corner behind the stove. Nobody else did anything either, just babbled to one another, talked on the phone, and on the radio.

Once they got excited. "B" Company was in a minefield and kept getting in another one and having lots of casualties. The mines were called "Bouncing Betties," if I remember right. When you tripped them they bounded in the air about crotch-level high and exploded. I don't even like to remember about them. I didn't last long in Headquarters. They took me back to my outfit in a jeep that night.

But now I'm in Headquarters all the time. I'm at least a General. My wife is still in the infantry and is on permanent kitchen police and latrine duty. I have awarded her an Expert Kitchen Badge and increased her allowance to five dollars a month. It's the least I could do.

My fellow Generals recently awarded me a medal for using the bathroom the least during an all-night beer party solving major problems. A life in Headquarters has many problems, but someone has to do it.

A Normal Childhood

<hr/>

Everybody blames their childhood for all their sins and faults. I can't do that because mine was like all the kids I knew. And I had a privileged childhood just like a lot of rich big shots. They are always bragging they were educated in Europe in private schools. So was I. I was even a private and had many tutors twenty-four hours a day. Most of the rich big shots were just in one country, but I went to school in many countries. I had to learn languages, customs, history, and cuisine all over Europe.

I walked everywhere, even ran a lot for a healthy childhood. I slept wherever and whenever I could. No blankets, pillow, or bed. You don't need all that. I slept on the floor for a long time after I could have been in a nice, soft bed.

Some of the things we were ordered to do take a little getting used to. Like being ordered to kill anyone that wasn't dressed like us. That's a lot of power to give kids, but we handled it very well. Of course, the other guys were ordered to kill you. So you had to pay attention twenty-four hours a day. You usually operated in pairs, so one of you had to be awake all night. Talk about a good night's sleep--you never got one. I was usually paired up with a new replacement. Until they got used to explosions, gun fire, and general uproar, all night they couldn't sleep; so I'd tell them to wake me if any Germans came close and I'd try to sleep.

I still remember a dream I had sixty-one years ago. I was sleeping in a foxhole and the Germans were shelling us. One big shell came really close and caused some of the dirt on the side of the hole to break loose and fall in my face. I woke dreaming that I was back home in bed during a summer thunderstorm.

Another time I was sleeping in a fox hole in the middle of a big, snow-covered field. My buddy woke me and said a lot of Germans were coming, for me to get on the automatic rifle and he'd shoot up a flare. I remember waking and in five seconds I was sighting down a gun barrel at a lot of legs moving against the white snow. The bodies blended with the dark woods behind them. The cold north wind was freezing my sighting eye. The flare went off and I saw a herd of deer that had been scared out of the woods and came toward us. Things like that will wake you right up better than a cup of good hot coffee. That's good, because we never had a cup of good hot coffee.

It was hard to get used to having your buddies get killed all the time. A lot of times we were within arms length and you had to see and hear them die. If we were attacking, you left them and went on just like they were a piece of garbage people throw out of a car window. Eventually all dead bodies were like garbage. They were everywhere and in the way. Try eating a can of pork and beans with a dead guy's brains lying on the ground in front of you. Damn garbage.

I don't want to drag out any more old memories right now explaining my childhood training.

Paris

I'VE LOTS OF MEMORIES OF PARIS besides its architecture, history, palaces, art museums, night life, and girls. It also had great customs. The last funeral procession I was in was not very long. No, it wasn't mine. Not only did traffic not stop, vehicles cut through at cross roads and big trucks even passed the procession. I don't think it had a police escort.

My main job in Paris was seeing that supplies were delivered to the many army headquarter units around town and there were many of them. Anyone who was anyone was stationed in Paris. Only the nobodies were in combat units.

One day I was with a Frenchman in his big truck going down a main street when he pulled to the curb and took off his hat. All the pedestrians had stopped and faced the street. Men took off their hats, and everybody had their hands over their heart. I asked the driver what was going on. He pointed down the street to an approaching hearse. I don't remember any procession and certainly no escort. It was just a French custom to honor the dead, and let them proceed with dignity in the few seconds it took. I was and am still impressed. I pull off the road and stop when I see a funeral procession. Sometimes I nearly get run over.

I remember this every time I hear or read what jerks and morons the French are for not always following our lead in world affairs. I'm not convinced the French are the only jerks and morons in the world. I was a soldier in Paris about seven months and I only remember two occasions when I was treated with disrespect. I'm disrespected more than that before breakfast anymore.

One time I was riding the Metro late at night and standing, leaning against the pole between the exit doors. The car was nearly empty. The car stopped and someone banged my shoulder with an umbrella. It was an old woman who didn't want to walk around me.

The other time I was riding a bus that had an old man with a long, white moustache who was a conductor. I hadn't been in Paris long and didn't know much of the language or accent yet. I wanted off at a stop spelled Baligny. I told the old man I wanted off at Bal-ig-knee. He turned red and screamed, "Ballinee" at me three or four times. I still remember how to pronounce it, if I ever go back.

I really don't know if I was disrespected or educated by a tired old teacher. If I live long enough and get enough ambition, I'll write more about one of the world's greatest cities—Paris.

The Quarry

—————

A LOT OF THINGS I would like to forget lie buried in my mind, crawling out every so often before I can push them back and bury them again. Maybe if I just let them out they won't bother me anymore. I'm going to try with a few.

This memory is about a rifle company that had just crossed the Rhine at Remagen in March 1945. We were expanding the bridge ahead by pushing the German Army back in a big half circle. We came upon a stone quarry in the woods, just exactly like stone quarries here in Monroe County, Indiana. The Germans had machine guns hidden in the rocks. It was next too impossible to even see them, let alone do anything about it. But we were given orders to attack them and drive them out.

Even as just soldiers, we thought it was crazy. Go around them, and they would have to surrender. Which was what eventually happened. But on this day, we attacked them. There was nothing to be gained or lost by who had the quarry. There was nothing lost but about twenty-five teenager lives.

This memory is about part of that day. About noon, the first platoon of about twenty-five soldiers were attacked across the quarry toward the stone stacks. The hidden machine guns mowed them down. You couldn't go get the wounded because anyone who tried got killed or wounded. We were just a few yards away and could hear the wounded very plainly.

One replacement we called Elephant Boy was hit and died there, but not before he cried for his mother for a long time. I don't remember his name. I'm sorry to call him Elephant Boy, but that's all I remember.

After a time, we thought the Germans had left, and the Army in its wisdom, ordered another attack. I was the scout who had to go first. I got to the edge of the quarry where I could see all the dead and wounded and hesitated awhile. To go in there was like a condemned man going to the electric chair—you were going to die.

Some officer behind me, who wasn't going with me, kept yelling for me to go on. I went, but not before I had a debate in my mind. I felt that I would probably die in this war anyway, and it might as well be here. I went to all the bodies, looking for one soldier still alive. I found one lying in a big pool of blood, who died later. His last conversation on earth was with me. I asked him if he knew where the Germans were. He said he thought they had left. He hadn't heard them talking for a while. I went on and soon discovered they hadn't. How I got out of there alive I'll never know.

We didn't take the quarry. We finally just went around it. And nothing was lost in the grand scheme of things but about twenty-five young lives.

From Popcorn Road to Paris and Back

<hr>

I THINK THERE IS an old saying, "You can take the boy out of Popcorn, but you can't take Popcorn out of the boy." I didn't always live on Popcorn Road. The fall and winter of 1945-46, believe it or not, I lived in Paris, France. I didn't just live there--I lived well. Had great friends, and still have great memories.

How I came to live there is an incredible story. I was in the Army after the end of WWII, and I was in Germany. But the war in Japan was still going on. Our lieutenant told us that we were going to make the invasion of Japan.

I had never been to Paris and it looked like I never would. I told myself, "What the Hell, I'm going. What's the Army going to do—kill me before the Japanese do?" So, I went to Paris. I cannot remember how many days I was gone, several I guess.

When I got back, my sergeant told me the captain wanted to see me immediately. I reported to the captain, saluted, and stood at attention. He asked me if I had been AWOL and I said, "Yes, sir!" He then asked me if I wanted a court-martial or ship out. I said, "ship out" as he knew I would.

He ordered me to get on that truck out front. I was sure it would go to a seaport and I would go to Japan. It drove and drove, and in the middle of the night stopped in front of a big hotel in downtown Paris. I was told to get out. I was to be stationed there.

Of course the captain knew where I was going for my punishment. I lived in a fancy hotel till I got a girlfriend, and eventually moved in with her. We ate dinner at her mother's house every night. Before dinner, I'd drink aperitifs and wine with dinner, followed by coffee and calvados. By then I was half drunk.

I noticed a U.S. Army staff car parked across the boulevard from my girlfriend's apartment. It was there every night. She told me last year a German Army staff car was parked there every night. She said none was ever parked in front of her apartment.

The Communist Party was very popular in Paris that year. My girlfriend liked it too, so I had to go to Russian nightclubs with Russian music and dancing. We also went to Russian movies with French subtitles. You are not going to find any of those on Popcorn Road.

One night when I was by myself, I met a beautiful, nude woman in high heels and an open fur coat. I cannot remember what we talked about, but I probably told her she should be ashamed wearing animal skin although I must say, she looked better in them than the animals themselves did.

About fifty years after that, Indiana University won some tournament or other and the paper said a nude woman in a fur coat was seen in Bloomington. I suppose there's hope for Bloomington yet. I never bought my wife a fur coat so probably I'll never see such a sight on Popcorn Road.

Seeing Eye to Eye

<hr>

It had been raining all night. We were marching single file along some road toward the Front. We were to take some town which was a jumping off point for the Rhine River.

We were all very quiet. I remember when we were going toward a battle, and we were always quiet--no talking, no joking, no laughing. Even the officers and non-coms were quiet, if they were good ones.

The battle was later written up in the Army newspaper, "Stars & Stripes." I sent the article home in a letter and found it the other day. It said General "Lightning Joe" Collins had taken the road junction and three divisions had gone through the hole in a race to the Rhine. I didn't see "Lightning Joe." I'm not saying he wasn't there. I just didn't see him.

What I saw were eighteen and nineteen-year-old kids. Most infantry companies were made up of teenagers. There must be a reason for that. Very important people made the decisions of what was to be done, but I left the doing to teenagers. I got a letter the other day from an old guy who was with me at the time. He said he had just turned twenty-one when he got out of the Army and had just started to shave.

I can remember during some inspection, an officer must have seen a wild hair on my face, for he said, "Did you shave this morning, soldier?" I said, "Yes, sir," and I'd never shaved in my life.

While we were marching in the dark and the rain along this road, we met a bunch of trucks, blacked out, full of German prisoners. The trucks were just creeping along and we were literally inches away from each other, looking each other in the eye. There was no talking, no laughing, nothing. We just looked at each other. They were just like us. Teenagers who probably had never shaved yet. The enemies we had been taught to hate were older, meaner, and vicious savages. They didn't look vicious or savage. It was a very strange experience, the conditions under which it happened. I will never forget it. They were going to safety as well as getting out of the mud and the rain. We were going, a lot of us, to our deaths. But we went, us Teenagers, and took the road junction the next morning and the tanks went through on the roads to the Rhine River.

And "Lightning Joe" Collins got the credit in the "Stars and Stripes." Like I said, I never saw him. But I'm not saying he wasn't there.

ADDICTIONS

I'M A VERY ADDICTIVE PERSON. I've been addicted to just about everything at one time or another.

When I was in the Infantry in Europe in 1944 through 1945, a few of my buddies and I were addicted to stress, danger, excitement, or what I would call, "cheating death." There is no bigger high than knowing you, or one, or the entire group should have been killed but weren't. You would laugh and joke after you had escaped death. It was better than winning the lottery. And, of course, there is no bigger downer than if one of you is killed. So why, if death weren't seeking us, we would seek it? But we did. Over and over again.

While the war was still on and it was quiet for a while, and there was something interesting in "no man's land," three or four of us would go to investigate it. We wouldn't ask permission, because we wouldn't have gotten it. We wouldn't tell anybody. We would just go. If we'd been killed, wounded, or captured, no one would have known. I wonder how many soldiers missing in action did something like that.

Germans don't live in isolated houses, except for hunting lodges in the mountains or castles scattered around. We were wandering around in "no man's land" once and discovered a hunting lodge. Among many things, it had food in it we would cook. Army K-rations would be all we had for weeks on end, mainly condensed cheese. It also had a wind up record player and lots of female German opera records. We would listen to opera for hours, and it was the most beautiful singing I've ever heard. I wonder how much the circumstances had to do with that.

When the war was over, we continued these idiotic acts. The Germans tried to set up a guerrilla movement in the southern mountains, which was where we were. They had hid arms in various places and intended to continue the war. One day a German civilian, who said he'd been a sergeant in the German Army in WWI, told us he knew of a cabin up in the mountains where arms were hid. He offered to take us there if we wanted to go. Silly man. Of course we wanted to go.

We left with him. Didn't tell anyone a thing. The mountain still had snow on it, and it soon started snowing hard. When the German said we were getting close, we all shut up and he directed us with what I'm sure were German Army hand signals. We understood them perfectly because they were the same ones we used. We surrounded the cabin and ordered the inhabitants out. Nothing happened, so we went in. No one was there, but the floor had been taken up and big holes had been dug. We were too late, and everything was gone.

But we'd had a lot of fun. It was long after dark when we got back. We learned later that the head of the Nazi SS lived in the area, so it made sense that the center of resistance would be there. We could have been led to slaughter and no one would have ever known. And the German was very brave, because we soon left there, and he may have had to pay a price for what he did. The same thing happened later in a different place with the same result.

I've lost that addiction now, along with most of my other ones. When I hear strange thumps in the night, I send my wife to investigate. Why should I have all the fun?

BLUE EYES

———❖———

WHAT IS IT ABOUT EYES? They're the first thing you look at when you meet someone. They're usually what you remember about someone. The pair of eyes I can't forget belonged to a young German boy in a little town near Kassel, Germany in April 1945.

Three or four of us American soldiers were holed up in a cellar in a little German town we had just taken, when the Germans counterattacked and tried to drive us out. Their tanks came in and drove our tanks out, but we were all in cellars and they didn't get us out. The tanks didn't have enough infantry with them.

A young dead German soldier was lying on his back in the cellar doorway. The doorway was very narrow and the steep, and narrow stairs went up just beyond the door. To get through the door you had to look down to see that you didn't step on the soldier's hands or arms, and all you could see were his bright blue eyes looking up at you. His eyes were covered with a film of dust.

We would say "Why don't one of you move him, I'm tired of him looking at me." But no one did and we soon left. I think his eyes bothered everyone the same as it did me. Why didn't we drag him out of the way? I don't know.

Why do his eyes still bother me? I don't know.

Was it the film of dust on them? I don't know.

IF YOU HAVE TROUBLE SLEEPING

It must be a normal reaction, as I get old enough to die. I think more about the times I should have died but didn't.

One experience I remember in particular because it had everything—ridiculous humor, danger, and eventually death for my buddy. It seems like I was on the outpost in the infantry every night. An outpost is a couple of guys sent out in the dark in front of our lines so if the enemy attacks, they will make enough noise killing the outpost that everyone will be woke and ready to go.

This happened close to the Rhine River up by Dusseldorf. My buddy, a new replacement from Pennsylvania (who was eighteen years old and full of life) and I were in front of our lines and had crawled into an old bomb hole for a foxhole. I did that a lot. Not only did it save digging a foxhole, but also I thought the odds were against another bomb falling in the same hole. I'm here now so I must have been right.

The night was totally black and you literally couldn't see your hand in front of your face. Suddenly, we heard German soldiers talking very close and followed by digging noises. The German Army had moved in.

I didn't know what to do. I was sure we would be discovered and killed any minute when suddenly an alarm clock went off in our bomb hole. My buddy started pawing in his ammo bag and finally shut it off. It seemed he had seen an interesting clock the day before and stuck it in his ammo bag.

Now I was sure we were dead, but the Germans just kept on talking and digging. The clock surely wasn't as loud as I thought or no German wanted to admit he heard an alarm clock. I can't remember how we got

29

out of that. I think the Germans just moved out. My blood pressure must have got so high it destroyed my memory.

The next day we had taken a little village when suddenly a few German tanks without infantry moved in and started shooting up the town. We dived into cellars and stayed there till they left. Then we started counting heads. My alarm clock buddy was missing.

We found him dead behind a house near some rabbit pens. It was spring and rabbit breeding time. If you've never seen rabbits breed, you don't know what sexual excitement is. They are hilarious. My buddy's hobby was mixing the sexes in German rabbit pens. He must have been laughing so hard at the rabbits he didn't hear us yell about the tanks.

I hope there are rabbits in heaven, but no alarm clocks, please.

Death of an Old Man

This is just the story of the useless, senseless, idiotic killing of an unknown, forgotten old man exactly when, where, and why I can't remember. It was a very small town, just a collection of a dozen houses, along a road in central Germany in the early spring of 1945.

I can only remember our squad, about seven or eight guys, being in a house on one end of the town. There were a few German soldiers in a house on the other end.

We were, as usual, completely worn out. We never really slept, just napped. I've went to sleep walking, and would stumble and wake up. I'm sure the nap only lasted a second, but I've never went to sleep walking since that period in my life.

The German soldiers, they were probably in as bad a shape as we were, so we all declared an unofficial truce. We would do that a lot. It just happened. The rules were very simple. We just ignored one another and rested, and tried to eat. It would last until some moron did something stupid, which always happened sooner or later.

The moron was usually an officer or non-com on either side who arrived and demanded we start killing each another. While the truce was in effect, an old man came up the road from the German end of the town.

I think he probably had Alzheimer's or was senile or something, or what was happening drove him out of his mind. He said the house we were in was his daughter's house, and he wanted to get something and carry it to his house, which was on the other end of town, where his daughter was.

He only got silly things, like an old chair, or a box of old shoes. He made several trips and then started carrying things both ways, and

31

finally alarmed someone in our group. The alarmed one must have been a replacement, because our old guys wouldn't be alarmed at what was happening.

The alarmed one wanted to shoot the old man. He said he was probably spying on us and telling the Germans where we were. We said don't be silly. Calm down and rest. The Germans know where we are.

Time passed. I think a moron arrived and wanted to know why we weren't killing one another. So the shooting started again. But the old man was still carrying things up the road. Then someone said somebody has shot the old man. He was lying dead in the road with an old kitchen chair in his arms. I don't know who shot him and no one is ever going to try to find out. It was just one of life's tragedies. We went on, ran the Germans out of town and went down the road to somewhere I don't remember.

All I can remember is the senseless killing of the old man.

SMALL SACRIFICES

I WATCH TOO MUCH TELEVISION.

I see generals, congressmen, cabinet members, presidents and other various professional blowhards blathering about sacrifice, duty, patriotism, etc. That's their right.

I have such a good memory. I was watching television about a tour up the Rhine River, with cliffside castles and other tourist attractions. Then I remembered my tour on the Rhine in late winter in 1945. I see black and white snapshots fly by in quick succession. I remembered being on the cliff top at Remagen, Germany. We had the first toe hold east of the Rhine. The Germans went all out to run us back over the river. I went through a battlefield one morning. I still have many pictures in my mind. The field was composed of many wheat fields that were already turning green.

The dead bodies were so thick you could step from body to body and never have to step on the ground. They were four or five to one German body, but there were plenty of American ones. They were all mixed up, three or four German bodies just a few feet from an American body.

It was obvious what had happened. The Germans were overrunning our infantry and would get back to our rear echelon and maybe throw us back over the river.

We had more artillery back across the river than anyone had ever seen before. They all fired shells with proximity fuses. These fuses were made in Bloomington, Indiana at the now departed RCA factory. My mother helped make them there.

You couldn't escape a proximity fuse shell. It was set to explode a few feet off the ground and would pretty much kill everybody under the explosion.

To keep the Germans from breaking through our infantry, it was decided at some higher headquarters back in the rear somewhere to use all that artillery with their proximity fuses and kill everyone—German and American. They succeeded.

The Germans didn't break through.

The next day I saw a few of the American survivors who were sacrificed there. They were in a little old school house, close to the edge of the cliff, that had miraculously survived all the shelling and bombing. They all had blank looks and stared straight ahead. I wonder if they ever recovered. I know too many infantry veterans who died very young from alcoholism. I know too many who died alone in their house and their bodies were found days later.

The survivors I saw were all little skinny, eighteen-year-old kids. They didn't know any powerful people or they wouldn't have been there. I'm sure their mothers got telegrams saying they were killed by enemy action.

No. They were sacrificed to save the bridgehead. I agree it was the right thing to do and saved lives in the long run. What I have trouble with is the fact that we always sacrifice eighteen-year-old boys who don't know any big shots. They were killed for a bigger cause; but were never recognized or awarded medals.

Can you imagine the fan fare, medals, and recognition if one of our professional blowhards would ever be sacrificed for a bigger cause?

I think that would make me swear off television forever.

LEGS

A PERFECTLY FORMED NUDE LEG, obviously female, was lying in the snow at the edge of the road. Its bare toes were sticking out by the snow, looking very cold.

It was the leg of a young woman that looked surgically removed. It was clean and white, had no bruises, cuts or scratches on it. Just lying in the snow. This happened in southeastern Belgium in late January of 1945. We were on our way to the front just across a little creek from the Seigfried Line. Why the leg was there was a total mystery. From its condition, I think it had to be intentionally cut off.

I was telling another old soldier about this the other day, and he said, "Well, you know there were a lot of criminals in the Army. You were always moving and could do what you pleased with the civilian population and not worry about being caught. It would be heaven for a serial killer." I remember though that the Germans had just been run off. The Battle of the Bulge was ending. So it probably was a German criminal.

I was talking on the phone to an old buddy who was there and he said he was glad he couldn't remember it.

When we got to the Front we occupied a German built log bunker dug into the hillside covered with dirt. It had a front door, bunks, and a stove. I suppose we would fire the stove too much sometimes and it would melt snow on top and ice cold snow water would drip on you.

There was something in German written on the door. With our trusty German American dictionary we learned it said, "The Everlasting Drip." A little town was out in 'No Man's Land,' and being young and needing constant excitement four or five of us went to explore it one day. Among other things we found a horse leg lying in a kitchen floor.

It was an entire rear leg removed at the hip. All the meat had been sliced off and the big long bone was just lying there.

It still had the horseshoe on. I've always thought they should have had the decency to remove the shoe. Obviously it had been eaten, whether by Belgian civilians or German soldiers. I don't know.

I've only got the equivalent of a leg and a half, so I'm very sympathetic to anyone or anything who has lost a leg. I can tell you two good legs are a lot better than one and a part.

I'll just tell one more leg story. This one is the worst because the victim was a soldier friend. We were removing our own antitank mines when one blew up and killed Ollie Olsen and blew one leg up in a tree.

We just left it there. We brought the body back to an old bakery we were holing up in. We laid the body by the front door and covered it with canvas.

I think it was still there when we left. I assume the Burial Detail guys got it and buried it sometime.

But his leg may still be in that tree. We should have gotten it down.

MEMORIES OF GUNGA DEAN

SOMEONE ASKED ME THE OTHER DAY why no one has nicknames anymore. I also wonder why no one hums or whistles anymore. I don't know, but I'll bet the answer will not be a credit to our society.

Everyone in the Army in the nineteen-forties had nicknames, including Wayne O. Dean. "Wayno," as he was known besides "Gunga," was a little stocky, cocky, loud kid from somewhere in Montana. We took Infantry basic together and went overseas together. We were in the same platoon, but different squads.

Infantry basic took place in northeast Texas, which was near Paris, Texas. Gunga and I went on a lot of weekend passes together in Texas and later in England. Late in the week Gunga would ask me if I wanted to go somewhere that weekend. I would say I didn't have any money. Gunga told me he didn't either but he had a checking account back in Montana.

All Texas towns had an American Legion bar. We would go in one, order a beer, and Gunga would say he needed to cash a check on his bank in Montana. The bartender would give him a blank check. Gunga would make it out for five dollars. The bartender would give him the money and we were on our way. If we ran out of money we would go in another bar and do it again. Five dollars went a long way in 1943. I don't think he had a checking account in Montana and I don't think any of those bartenders believed he had a checking account, but they cashed his check anyway.

Texas was a very patriotic place and I think Gunga discovered an American Legion bar would cash a soldier's personal check if it wasn't very big. So we left a string of bad five-dollar checks across Texas, Oklahoma, and Arkansas. Maybe, maybe not. I don't know. He could have had a checking account. All of them probably didn't total fifty dollars. You didn't need much money then. We hitchhiked everywhere we went. We liked to find a little town that wasn't full of soldiers. If we had a few dollars we went to Ada, Oklahoma a couple of times.

If we were totally broke and just had to get away from the Army for a while we would hitchhike to Hugo, Oklahoma on Sunday. There was a big ice house there and the night watchman would let us in. We would set on a cake of ice and eat watermelon the watchman gave us. These were hot Texas nights and when we were cooled off we would hitchhike back to camp and start another week.

My funniest memories of Gunga happened on a weekend pass in London and our first night in combat. It's very hard to remember details of fifty-four-year-old memories. I think on a Friday morning we crossed southern England by train from Dorchester to London, stopping at every little town. We did all the things in London any proper tourist would do, but being soldiers who knew we would be in infantry combat in a few days, we also did things any proper tourist wouldn't do.

For instance we were in Westminister Abbey Sunday morning during church services. I can remember standing on Sir Isaac Newton's grave during services. Famous people were buried in the floor. But the night before we were a long way from Westminister Abbey, London was blacked out which made things more interesting for people like us.

During our travels we were accosted by a Cockney lady of the night. She was back in a doorway and turned a flashlight on under her chin. I think she asked if we were looking for a good time. Gunga told her we were, but not with the likes of her. That did it. She really got mad and followed us down the street listing all our attributes in that Cockney accent. When she was about to go on her way, Gunga would insult her again and everything would start over again. Her parting shot was that we would see the day when we would get on our knees to kiss her arse.

Maybe a week later we were together in a fox hole one night in our first combat experience. We were really scared. We were sure every shell would land on us. Nothing even came close.

A few weeks later we would have slept through the whole thing. We were veterans then and knew what to be afraid of. But this night we were afraid of everything. We wouldn't talk for hours, just look and listen. Once we wondered if we ought to shoot one another in the leg and we weren't entirely kidding. After one long silence Gunga said, "you know I would get on my knees to kiss her arse." That helped a lot.

My last memory of Gunga isn't so funny. We were both looking out a second story window of a house when a mortar shell hit a tree top just outside. A piece of shrapnel hit him in the forehead. He fell and kicked for a few seconds and bloody froth came out of his ears and nose, and he lay still.

This last memory is not the one I would have chosen, but it's the one I'm stuck with.

Ambulance Rides I Have Taken

THE OTHER DAY I PASSED OUT for the first time in my life, while I was sober, anyway. I knew I was feeling awful, and was sitting in my car talking to a minister by the Harrodsburg Post Office. When I came to, he was praying for me. Someone called an ambulance and they took me to the Emergency Room.

After two days of many tests and examinations, they told me to drink more water. I told them that when I could afford something else, I would quit drinking water. One day they hooked about twenty wires to my head and watched my brain activity. They saw nothing. I could have told them that.

On my way to the hospital I remembered the other two times I rode in an ambulance. One time was twenty years ago when I got run over by my own tractor. It happened early in the morning, and no one knew where I was. I knew no one would even look for me till about nine that evening, and they didn't. That was the longest, hardest day of my life. The ambulance took me to the Emergency Room about midnight, and the ambulance crew was the most "anticipated" people I have ever met in my life.

The third ambulance trip happened fifty-eight years ago. It just popped into my memory. It happened during the Battle of the Bulge in 1944. We were constantly in the snow and were wet all the time, including shoes and socks. We didn't have overshoes, just leggings, which were canvas and leaked water like a sieve. I don't remember ever getting overshoes. I'm sure the rear echelon people in London and Paris needed them more. I dried my socks by putting them on my belly under my shirt. It was a very pleasant experience when you were outside all the time.

One morning after spending all night in a wet snow, I was sick as a dog. The platoon medic (God bless his soul), said I had pneumonia and sent me to the rear. The German Army was attacking everywhere. The ambulance driver would tell me to look up to my right or left and there would be German and American planes in a dogfight. Other German planes were bombing and strafing.

The roads were jammed with Belgian civilians going to the rear. They were on foot; they didn't have vehicles, and wouldn't have had fuel if they did. They were taking great-grandma, babies, and what possessions they could on their backs in the snow. They wouldn't even look at us and I don't blame them. I admired the Belgians more than any other Europeans.

The Germans came through their country in 1940, looting and destroying. We came through Belgium just a few weeks before this, and Belgium was destroyed again. The civilians would hug and kiss us, give us wine and cognac, and Victory signs, and we let them down. Here came the Germans again, looting and destroying. And in a month we came back through Belgium, driving the Germans out and again redestroying what was already destroyed. If Belgium were a wine, nobody would have wanted the 1944 vintage.

The ambulance, under blackout conditions, finally came to a stop in the dark. The doors were flung open and dark figures, speaking German, started pulling my stretcher out. I knew I had been captured and since I couldn't walk far I would probably be shot. But I soon learned that they were POWS' working as hospital orderlies.

The hospital was several tents standing in the snow near Liege, Belgium. Liege had railroad yards that supplied our Army. At that time, the Germans had what we called "buzz" bombs, which were big rockets with a pulse-jet engine. When the rocket was close to its target the engine would shut off and then it would glide into the target. The Germans would send a rocket every few minutes trying to destroy the supply dump. A rocket engine was shutting off near our tent every few minutes, night and day.

When you heard the engine shut down, you held your breath till it exploded and you were safe for a few more minutes. The night nurse in our tent was terrified of them and would cry all night. They should have sent her farther to the rear, back somewhere where they wore overshoes.

I just stayed there two or three days; they filled me full of penicillin and sent me back to the front. They must have done a good job because I've never had pneumonia since. I've never lain in a snow bank all winter since then either.

Before I got back to my squad, I had a short and incomplete memory so full of symbolism I don't need to explain it. The memory is like a sharp black and white photograph. I have a partial memory of getting out of a truck just at dawn; someone must have given me a rifle and pointed to where my squad was. I started toward them and was in a large, open snow-covered field. Suddenly a German fighter plane popped up out of the valley below and came straight toward me. It was flying just a few feet off the ground. When it was a few feet away, the pilot tipped it up on one wing and we made eye contact as he went by and disappeared. My memory ends there for that period of time.

CHRISTMAS IN FRANCE

FOLLOWING IS A STORY ABOUT an Army Christmas. I can't remember a thing about 1943 or 1944. New Year's Eve in 1944 I do remember we were still in Hofen and I was at an outpost with someone I don't remember. It was a clear, cold, quiet night, the kind that sound carries a long way. At midnight, in the distance someone played a shave and a haircut...two bits... on his machine gun. He was very good. That's all I remember about the New Year.

During Christmas of 1945, I was stationed in Paris with a very good job. I think I was supposed to have gone home, but I kept missing the boat. Finally, the Army told me to catch the next one or else. But during Christmas in 1945, I was still in Paris. A French family I knew asked me to go with them to a little town in Normandy where they were originally from. We had to change trains three or four times and walk the last several miles to get there. The area had been fought over, and the ditches were full of grenades, bazookas, ammo of all kinds (mainly German). There were signs in French, "Danger! Stay Out!" Along the road, there were tanks that had been destroyed, both U.S. and German.

The little town was named Coulee Boeuf. It didn't seem to be torn up much or they had done a lot of repairing. We stayed in a house that had survived three generations of families. The floors were of fieldstone, and there was only enough heat for cooking. I, of course, was use to far much worse conditions.

Coulee Boeuf didn't have a church, but the next town did. Just before dark, most of the townspeople walked in the snow (between the ditches full of explosives) to the next town to attend the Christmas

Mass. It was very cold, because I can remember hearing the snow squeak when you walked.

The church was very old and dark, with no heat. The back half of the church was filled with German soldiers in uniform. I didn't see any guards. I assume they were there to clean up all the shells, mines, and so forth. After Mass, we all walked back to Coulee Boeuf and had what I was told a traditional meal before Christmas. I don't remember what we ate.

What I do remember was that it was the same cast as Christmas during 1944, but so different. If you can explain this to me, I'd like to hear it.

IN THE SERVICE OF OUR COUNTRY

AT THE END OF WWII in Europe, I was somewhere in the vicinity of the Danube River in southeast Germany, or maybe Austria, I don't remember which. We had been told we probably would go to the Far East to help defeat Japan, so we weren't really celebrating that much.

There were idiots in high places in government then also. Some member of President Roosevelt and Truman's Cabinet, on his own, issued an order proclaiming Germany was to be made a nation of goat herders; never to be a world power again. He also said soldiers could not fraternize with German civilians. He meant girls. Violators would be court-martialed, he said. He was certainly a brilliant man.

Our C.O., who was a good officer, got the company together and read the new rule to us. He said he would not go out looking for us fraternizing, but if he was taking a walk, and fell over us fraternizing, he would have to do something about it. He then told us where he took walks. You don't find many officers like him.

We were assigned areas to oversee during the immediate occupation of Germany. Our platoon, about thirty soldiers, was assigned an area about the size of a township, I think. We spent most of our time in a little town on a narrow, deep, swift, cold river. They used the river to power a small electric generating plant. There was a one-lane bridge across the river right below the power plant.

We went swimming in the nude there nearly every afternoon. A German soldier who had returned home, still in uniform, would swim with us. Civilians, mainly girls, would stand on the bridge and watch us while doing a lot of finger pointing and giggling. It didn't take much pointing and giggling to make a guy like me stay in that cold water till I nearly froze.

The Army, in its wisdom, knew they had to keep us teenagers busy or we would start associating with loose women and drink alcohol, of which there was a lot around. The little town made both beer and schnapps. I used to say they made us guard manure piles in the rain. We also had to guard the electric plant. It was right on the river and made a lot of noise. Across the street in front was a high stone wall with a road that made a sharp turn right at the front of the plant, so a vehicle could be right on you before you could see or hear it.

I had a girlfriend named Elsa, who had been in the German Army in the occupation of Yugoslavia. She worked in a telephone exchange in some headquarters in the Army. She showed me pictures of herself in her uniform of which she was very proud. And why not. She would stand guard with me at the power plant, especially after dark, and there weren't any night lights.

One night I was on guard, my rifle on a sling on my shoulder, a cigarette in my mouth, my left arm around Elsa's neck, a bucket of beer in my right hand; which Elsa's little brother had just brought us from the brewery, when around the corner popped a jeep with my C.O.

I had to do some quick thinking. I didn't want to spill the bucket of beer, so I just raised my left arm off Elsa's neck and saluted the C.O. with my left hand, a cigarette in my mouth, and beer in my right hand. My C.O., laughing hard, saluted back, and kept going. I can't remember if he used his left hand or not.

You can see that duty in far away, foreign places, is a hard, cold, lonesome task; but someone had to do it.

I'VE BEEN PRIVILEGED

FOR A KID BORN AND RAISED at the end of a long mud road, I've been to a lot of places and done a lot of things. When you were raised during the Depression, you had a lot of dreams, but your expectations weren't very high.

We had a battery radio, but the battery was usually dead. Also, we had no television, newspapers, magazines and usually no phone. My contact with the world was through the library truck that came by once a month at the end of the mud road. You walked out with all your books and waited until it came along. It was just a pickup truck with a few shelves of books. I always got the limit, whatever it was, and read everything worth reading on the truck over time. I complained to the library lady once that I had read all her books. She replied, "Oh, surely not!"

We never went anywhere. I was never close to being out of the state. And then I was in the Army. I immediately left the state for Little Rock, Arkansas where I took medical basic training. Then the Army sent me to the University of Arkansas at Fayetteville. The Army put me in the Infantry and sent me to Europe.

For someone who had never been anywhere, I was now a world traveler. The first time I saw the ocean I got in a boat and crossed it. I then backpacked Europe—England, France, Luxembourg, Belgium, Germany, and Austria.

I didn't spend any money, ate what I could find in cellars, robbed chicken nests, shot cattle, and ate the crap the Army gave me—mainly K-rations. I slept everywhere—in beds, hotels, barn lofts, basements, but mainly woods and fields.

That's the only way to learn about a country. You can't learn anything just going from airports to the Day's Inn Motel. I didn't like beds and pillows for a long time after—I'd just sleep on the floor.

I had some rewarding experiences—crossing the ocean in a huge convoy with submarine alerts keeping you on your toes, seeing London in blackouts, wading ashore in France in the middle of the night.

The World's leaders were really something then also--Roosevelt and Truman in the U.S., and Churchill in England. I was in Germany for seven months while Hitler was in charge. I used to get drunk with the Russians when Stalin was the dictator and several years later I was in China while Mao was the great Helmsman.

I got to see airplane fights up close, and was just across the Rhine one night when the RAF firebombed Dusseldorf. Once I was up on a high hill when a big infantry, tank, artillery, and dive-bomber battle went on below me. It was better than the drive-in theater, but it did kind of ruin going to the Fourth of July fireworks.

Once we took a town that was holding up the war—all the roads ran through it. After we took it, I was sitting in the mayor's office looking out the window while two divisions (20,000 men) went by on the street outside to attack the Germans. Now the mayor wouldn't let me in his office.

It was a great privilege to have done all these things. But the biggest privilege is being seventy-seven years old when I know I should have been dead at twenty.

A Close Call

ON DECEMBER 15TH, 1944, the night before the "Battle of the Bulge" began, I had been on night patrol as a scout walking five miles towards the German border and back to my platoon. On this particular night, while on my way back with five other soldiers, I heard someone whistle and looked up to see a German soldier about 6 feet above me on an embankment. He was dressed in white. Our eyes met, but I didn't stop walking or say anything to my fellow soldiers. I didn't know what to do. I make a split-second decision to just ignore him and keep walking as I didn't know if he and the other soldiers in the woods were going to kill us or not.

I also spotted other German soldiers dressed in white camouflage walking through the woods as this was winter and there was snow on the ground. The soldier who whistled at me must have thought we were German soldiers who had just crossed the Belgium border from Germany as we were walking back in the direction of our platoon. I had a feeling this German who whistled at me was an SS Officer. I don't know if he was suspicious since I didn't respond with a salute, or acknowledge him in any way. He must not have been able to recognize the shape of my helmet as I looked upward at him. You would think he had to know we weren't German. We weren't in white camouflage either. I still don't know how we were so lucky to have made it back to our platoon. I can only assume again that a bigger presence was watching over me.

When I told my commanding officer and fellow soldiers who had been on patrol with me what had happened, they didn't believe me. So another group of soldiers were sent out that same night to check this out and they never returned. I am sure they were shot. The next day was the beginning of the Battle of the Bulge.

When I was a Bad Ass

I'VE NOT ALWAYS BEEN such a sweetheart like I am now. Believe it or not, back when I was nineteen, I could be a real jerk. I remembered an incident when I was in the infantry in Germany in 1945.

We had been chasing a German Army horse outfit for hours. We were riding on tanks, so you could say we should have caught them easily. However, they would leave a gun behind every now and then. When we came around a turn on a hillside or went over a hill top, they would fire on us. It would be hard to knock the gun out, so the horses would get a good head start.

I remember once that day I was lying near some trees, and an antitank gun laid a shell right beside me. The explosion was so forceful that I remember it nearly rolled me over. Just before dark we finally caught up with them in a small town with a high embankment and a railroad on top. The only way out of town was through a narrow tunnel under the railroad. We were smarter than Indians chasing a stagecoach for hours but not catching anything. We shot the horses in the tunnel and captured the outfit.

I remember a young, beautiful girl had run out to see what was going on. A piece of shrapnel hit her leg, and she was bleeding and screaming. All the medicine the infantry carries with them is the PFC medic with some band aids and anti-infection pills. Poor little girl. Things like that happened around us all the time.

At nighttime, I couldn't sleep because I kept hearing the horses. They were still hooked up to various things and some had been wounded. I had been raised around horses on a farm, so I got up and unharnessed them, letting them run free. I decided to then check out the wagons. One was a two-wheeler holding a huge cooking pot/

furnace combination which enabled them to cook on the move. They had been cooking split-pea soup. I didn't eat any of the soup.

Checking around some more, I then found the headquarters wagon. It had the best automatic pistol I had ever laid eyes on. I also found in the wagon a large, metal box with the payroll inside. I found fresh German money with the bands still holding them. Quickly, I filled up the pockets of my field jacket and my pants till they could hold no more. What I did with the money will take a few more stories.

The next day my buddy and I were walking around the town. We discovered a huge factory that had not been damaged, so we went inside to check it out. No one was around, except for the manager. He showed us his credentials, all the while telling us how important he was, that we should leave and not damage anything. I sure wouldn't want to have worked for him. He sat in his chair at a big desk, in his big office, with a big glass picture of Hitler hanging on the wall behind him.

The manager was such a creep. I couldn't stand him, so I pulled out my new pistol and told him I hadn't fired it yet. I emptied the gun, aiming at the glass picture. The glass flew all over the creep, and his big desk. It's amazing how fast creeps can turn into sweethearts like me. But he did.

I know a few creeps I would like to treat the same way—some who let me know how they despise soldiers, especially lowlife moron infantry soldiers, like me. If I wasn't such a sweetheart, they would be covered with flying glass.

I wonder if a sweetheart can turn back into a real, bad ass jerk.

In My Dreams

—⟫◆⟪—

EVERYONE HAS HAD CLOSE CALLS in death or serious injury in their lifetime, but I think I've had more than my share. And I cannot forget them.

This one happened in early December, 1944, just inside the German border from Belgium near a little German town called Hofen. I can only remember two of us in a foxhole on our outpost, but I read an old letter I had sent home about this incident which I had reported there were three of us. I cannot remember the third guy, but the other one I remember very well. He was Jim Underwood of West Virginia. I probably owe my life to how Jim handled our problem. However, first I have to explain a few details.

Someone had dug a foxhole similar to a groundhog hole into the side of a bank on a little narrow road running straight east into Germany with a hedgerow beside it. After digging into the bank, the hole created a small cave where two guys could sleep while the third was on guard. Another hole had been dug straight up into the hedgerow so the guard could stand up and look out. A box had been put over the hole with an opening so one could look east toward the German lines. There was barbed wire strung across the road with the only opening right over the hole into the bank. Finally, an old barn door had been placed over the hole to keep out the wind and the snow. This was pure genius thinking. Any fool knows the enemy could only come down that road from the east. Right? I did not have anything to do with all that great thinking. I was just in there standing guard.

During the night, we had a blizzard that also helped save my life as it blew snow over the barn door. I was sleeping while Jim took his turn on guard. He woke me up and told me that Germans were everywhere outside our hole. That really got my attention, and I was desperate to solve the problem. I got on our sound power phone which was always on, never rang, and you hissed into it to get attention on the other end. Hissing like a rattlesnake, I told the answerer behind us in platoon headquarters our problem and to send up a flare. He did, and while I was looking out the hole I just saw the leg of one German running through a hole in the hedgerow. Any combat soldier would recognize the sound of the flare and do his best to disappear.

The blizzard quit during the night, and we back-tracked the Germans. They had wandered around everywhere behind our lines, and walked across our barn door from the rear. The snow had covered our barn door, Jim did not do anything foolish, and we all lived another night. That is all anyone could have asked.

I still remember a dream I had in that same hole, maybe that same night, sometime in December of 1944. Again, I was sound asleep when a lot of German artillery shells started landing close by my foxhole. I woke up dreaming I was back home in my bed during a summer thunderstorm.

Thank God for dreams.

THESE LITTLE THINGS I REMEMBER

THESE LITTLE THINGS I REMEMBER because they were funny, or incredible, or just important to me. I will not verify that the spelling of names or even the country where it happened is correct, but the incidents did happen.

In 1944 in England, I went to an English movie once. The newsreel showed the British Army killing a German soldier. Everyone in the theater, nearly all women and children, jumped up, cheered and whistled, and clapped. They were a little closer to things than our civilians.

One Saturday we were taking our daily ten-mile run, when a daily English shower started falling. We were in the middle of a little English town full of women and children. Without even thinking, we took condoms out of our pockets and pulled them down over our rifle barrels. Two things you didn't want to do in the infantry—get a venereal disease or have a rusty rifle barrel. What a sight that must have been—200 soldiers putting condoms on their rifles. The women didn't turn away--they put their hands over their faces with their fingers spread wide and giggled.

I think after the war, somewhere in Germany, a wise butt kid from New York took me to a play featuring the married couple Alfred Lunt and Lynn Fontaine, the most famous stage actors in the country at that time. After the curtain dropped we went backstage to congratulate the actors. He said that's what a New Yorker did. I think I was kissed by Lynn Fontaine, but I don't remember Alfred showing much concern.

Another time, in a little German town with a river running through it, I saw an incredible sight. Early in the morning a man came down the road with a herd of geese in tow. He would stop at every barnyard gate, open it and let two or three geese out to join the throng. They would all noisily say good morning to each other. Then they continued down the road, repeating things at every gate. They then would all go to the river and stay all day. Just before dark, here they came back up the road, stopping at every gate and letting the geese who lived there go inside for the night.

As a soldier, I have marched in review for many generals, including Eisenhower and Patton. I don't remember anything about it, except that it was a real pain. I didn't feel honored or appreciated, it was just something I had to do.

But once in Belgium, just after the Battle of the Bulge, our company passed in review for four or five Army nurses. I'll always remember that as the highest honor I ever received. It was just at dark, snowing hard, when we came out of the woods and went down a narrow Belgian road. We went by a two-story building with a balcony that the Army was using as an aide station. Four or five nurses came out and cheered us as went by.

That was as good as it ever got.

To All Mothers

———⟩⟩●⟨⟨———

THIS LETTER IS FOR all mothers everywhere. I've always thought a mother's love is the strongest force in the world and I'm becoming more convinced all the time.

My father died March 10, 2002. He was 103 years old. People commented on how far his mind was wandering in his last days and hours. I told them it was on a longer chain than ours.

When his mind returned from its last journey, he asked my sister if she knew when his mother was coming to see him.

His mother died ninety-eight years ago when he was five years old.

Homer Barrett's Gate

Starbucks, sprawl, golf courses, traffic calmers, and I-69. Our media, politicians, and leading intellectuals seem to be overwhelmed at all of these problems.

I think my long dead grandfather would have had solutions. For example, the WPA in 1935 started widening Popcorn Road. They just used picks, shovels, and wheelbarrows. We hadn't learned to wear hardhats and stand around watching backhoes yet. Grandfather said widening Popcorn Road so two wagons could pass one another was the biggest waste of money he had ever seen.

There never had been nor ever would be enough traffic on Popcorn Road to warrant making it two lanes. Even if you ever met another wagon you could pull over at Homer Barrett's gate and let it go by. Homer is not around anymore, but his gate is still there. We can still pull over and let the wagon go by.

But grandfather was right, I can't remember ever seeing two wagons passing on Popcorn Road. However, widening the road brought in a lot more people, all foreigners, I think, because they all drive on the wrong side of the road. If widening Popcorn Road caused these problems, think what I-69 will do. We'll have to have at least one more planning board to handle the demand for more traffic calmers, golf courses, and Starbucks.

I've heard Donald Trump may come to get in on the sprawl.

I think grandfather would say Homer Barrett needs to build a few more gates so we can pull over and wait, till Donald Trump gets by, at least.

HORSE SENSE

———◦◦◦———

SINCE OUR WORLD SEEMS balanced on a razor's edge—girls climbing trees to slay giants like Jack and the Beanstalk...the most powerful nations quibbling about "sorry" and "very sorry" to settle quarrels—we need something simple to think about.

My grandfather said that in 1905 he was running his cane press to make sorghum molasses. He was inside a little shed feeding cane stalks into the rollers to squeeze the juice out. His horse was outside, hooked to a pole, walking in a circle, powering the press. Suddenly, the horse stopped and refused to go on, despite all his yelling and threats.

He finally went outside to give it a good switching and discovered my future mother, who was just learning to walk, had wandered over there and sat down in the path the horse had to use. The horse used his "horse sense" and solved the problem.

My grandfather had tears in his eyes as he told me about it, and I have tears in mine as I write about it. Old horse, wherever you are, I'm very, very sorry that we questioned your good sense.

Now we can all get back to more "important" things.

Are you Afraid of the Dark?

IF YOU ARE UNDER SIXTY-YEARS OLD, you probably don't know. You've never been in the dark. Oh…you've been in the bathroom with the lights out with the door shut, but probably a crack of light was coming under the door.

Today, there is no real darkness. Cities in the distance look like a sunrise, and everyone in the country has lights on all night. Also, nobody sees ghosts anymore, and we laugh about old timers and their ghost stories. Old timers lived when the nights were really dark, and you couldn't tell what you saw.

When I was young, I worked till midnight. I would come home, park the car on the road, and walked around to the back of the house in the dark. I then ate a little bit, read the paper, and went to bed.

Back then, when people died, they would bring the body home. Friends and neighbors stayed with the body twenty-four hours a day until the funeral. We had neighbors down the road who had a death and friends stayed all night. They came over to the house one morning and told us we had a ghost. Every night, about one o'clock in the morning, a dim light came on in the kitchen and a ghost sat at the table a long time without moving.

I can't laugh at that because, shortly afterwards, I came home from work, and walked around to the back of the house. On this night, it was really, really dark outside. I made out a big, black figure lying in the middle of my path. I couldn't tell what it was. The hair stood up on the back of my neck and I wanted to run the other way…but my wife and kids were in the house.

My first thought was that it might be a cow that had gotten out and was now lying in the path. I stomped my foot and yelled. Nothing happened.

It was a ghost, a dragon, or something that was really evil. I screamed, running toward this dark form, and then kicked the Hell out of it.

Earlier that day, my wife had thrown out the Christmas tree.

Old Men

THERE ISN'T ANY NEED for old men anymore. They used to be prized for their wisdom and knowledge. But, as we all know and have been told repeatedly, all true knowledge and wisdom can now be found on the internet.

I believe to be wanted and needed is one of the basics for happiness and a good life. I think that is true for everyone, including children.

What caused me to think on this line is the sixty-year-old memory of an old barn. It was a very old barn in 1935. It sat on a high hill and took the full force of the wind. It was tall for a barn in those days and was built with wooden beams put together with big wooden pegs. It had a wooden shingle roof, the kind that you made yourself on the site.

I remember the roof because when I was very young I had to help take the old shingles off and replace them with a tin roof. I'll bet I was stung a hundred times by wasps and mud daubers. You just had to take it because of the fear of falling off the high and very steep roof.

The barn had a hay fork in it that ran on a track at the peak of the roof and was pulled by a big rope. One of my first jobs was riding a horse that pulled the rope that got the hay in the barn. It was a perfect illustration of being wanted and needed. I also got yelled at a lot. That goes with being wanted and needed.

That old barn, in 1935, was leaning and because it was wanted and needed, something had to be done. One Saturday morning my father invited all the old men in a three-mile radius to meet at the old barn and figure out a way to fit ix.

He invited all the ones with good sense, but you had to invite the ones without any sense at all because they would be mad when they found they had been left out.

It worked. They figured out what needed to be done and straightened the barn. It's still standing sixty-three years later. But what I really remember is how much fun the old men had that morning. They laughed and joked and told stories while they worked. I doubt if they even got paid anything, and if they did, it didn't amount to much. I think they just enjoyed being wanted and needed.

The old men have all been dead for many years. I noticed the other day that the old barn is beginning to lean again. Oh well. I'm sure the internet has the answer.

THE GOOD OLD DAYS

LOTS OF PEOPLE LIKE TO TALK about the good old days—politicians especially—and some old people when talking to the younger generation.

If my memory is any good, anyone who talks about the good old days probably wasn't there, or is a liar, a fool, or suffering from senility, or all of the above. Especially politicians.

If having no material goods, entertainment, food variety, travel, electricity, dental or medical care was good—then I lived in the good old days.

Except for Sunday shoes, kids went barefoot till the snow flew. Any kind of new clothing was an absolute necessity. An old aunt, with a boy a year older than I, gave me her son's only suit to wear at my high school graduation. I can't remember if I had to give it back or not.

We used to go to tent revivals for entertainment. My friends and I would sit up front at the side of the altar and judge the preachers by how high they could jump and how far they would spit while preaching. We also liked to hear people testify. Even then we understood that the real sinners sat in pious silence while the dumber ones confessed to their sins. Some things never change.

I could write a book on this subject but for now I'll just hit some highlights. No electricity and no refrigerator, and since we lived at the end of a long, mud road, there was no ice in our icebox except for special occasions. We used a spring down over a steep hill as both a "refrigerator" and, as our local paper is always saying, 'our sole source of drinking water.' But if you have a small boy with nothing to do, he can always run back and forth to the spring putting things in or getting things out of the "refrigerator" and bringing back a bucket of cold water in his idle hand. At that time I was a small boy with nothing to do.

They say Lincoln freed the slaves in 1865, but small boys weren't freed until electricity came to our area in 1946. When we put food or drink in the spring we used cans and buckets with lids to keep out raccoons, possums, dogs, snakes, frogs, and many other things. If we were gone and it came a big rain, it would wash our cans and buckets down the creek. If we wanted any supper, small boys had to run down the creek and find all the cans and buckets before they got to the Gulf of Mexico. I'm firmly convinced small boys were the main force behind civilization, as we know it.

Medicine was another wonderful thing in the good old days. We didn't have Blue Cross or Medicare, but we did have small boys with nothing to do. One cold winter night my mother was really sick and since we had a phone with a party line that worked that night, my father called our old doctor. I can't remember if he was still in Harrodsburg or had moved to Bloomington. Anyway, the doctor came to give my mother something that made her feel better for a while. My father said he didn't have any money but what could he give the doctor for payment. The doctor said, "Give me a couple of chickens."

As a small boy, with nothing to do, I lit the lantern and went to the hen house, put two chickens in a gunnysack, and put them in the doctor's car. It was a lot easier than filling out a bunch of insurance forms.

Another time my sister lay at death's door one whole summer. You can imagine the doctor bill. Since my father didn't have any money, but did have a small boy with nothing to do, the doctor said I could stay at his house and work for him till the bill was paid.

The doctor had a farm where College Mall is now located in Bloomington. I lived and slept in the attic and worked on his farm during the day. They had a maid, a refrigerator, ice, and many other things I wasn't used to having. At meal times the maid would say, "Bobby, what do you want to drink?" My choices were ten kinds of soda pop, lemonade, iced tea, and ginger ale, a drink that I had never heard of. They never knew whether I really worked or not but at home they sure did, and on rainy days I got to ride their bicycle into Bloomington. I hoped the doctor bill would never be paid, but they finally decided to send me back home. No more maid saying, "Bobby, what would you like to drink?"

I am old, crippled man now, and I really miss the good old days.

Have a Cookie

I'M GLAD I'VE ALWAYS liked old people. So few people do, so they're grateful for little things, such as taking the time to listen to their stories of how things were. At the age of four or five, I would visit old people in the neighborhood and they would tell me stories of how things were in 1860. Also, they usually gave me a cookie.

Of course, none of them were very important. The people I know now must be very important, they seem to carry the burden of the world on their shoulders. But they don't have time to listen to my stories of how things were in 1930. I don't give them a cookie, either.

My grandfather told me stories of how things were when he was a boy before the Civil War and Custer's Last Stand. I was watching him shock oats once behind a horse drawn binder, the latest improvement in agriculture. He told me what a great improvement that was. When he was a boy he cut oats with a scythe and cradle. A healthy, strong man on a good day could cut an acre a day, he told me.

I was watching my skinny sixteen-year-old grandson cut the other day with the latest improvement in that type of machine. He could cut an acre in fifteen minutes--without even trying. Whether you like it or not, our society is based on the fact that we can cut an acre of oats in fifteen minutes instead of a day.

I hope someone develops something to improve how we spend the time we save. Maybe we just need to listen to old people tell us how things were.

And get a cookie.

How Tony Thrasher Has
Lived to be 100

(date of story: 1/1999)

TONY WAS BORN CLOSE to Cedar Bluff Road north of Harrodsburg on February 28, 1899. That's really the secret to being a hundred years old. He was born a hundred years ago. If you were born a hundred years ago, you would be a hundred, too.

Other things enter into it, of course. He's outlived most of his doctors. Every so often one of them has given him just a few more months to live. He wouldn't pay them and they would always give him more time. Try it, he says it works.

Sixty-five years ago I remember him bragging about how he and his buddies would run down the road when school was out and hide in the weeds and moon the sweet little girls when they went by. He said they would run off screaming, in a panic. I can understand that. Now he says he can't remember that happening. We need to find someone who went to School No. 5 in 1906 and find out what really happened, maybe appoint an independent counsel.

I don't know what it means, but he has never eaten, exercised, or medicated properly. For at least ninety-years he had a diet of fried pork, biscuits and gravy, and plenty of real butter and cream.

But he's always liked to play jokes on people. Years ago Claude McGlothin had a hog butchered. Tony asked if he could borrow a ham till he butchered. Claude gave him one. Time passed. Claude wanted to know when he was going to butcher. Tony said he didn't know, he didn't have a hog.

And, of course, everything was a lot tougher in the old days. In 1905, when he had to walk 12 miles to school, snow was on the ground the entire school year and you had to walk uphill, both coming and going.

But I think the real secret to living a hundred years is having a lot of hobbies. Tony's hobby in the winter was cutting wood with a crosscut saw. In the spring, it was hauling manure. In the summer, it was putting up hay with a pitchfork. In the fall, it was shucking corn by hand. That's probably why none of us are one hundred years old. We don't have any good hobbies like that. You can't say too much for hobbies, you know.

This time next year, Tony will have lived in three centuries. That may not be a record, but it's sure a good average.

[Tony was Robert's father, who passed away at the age of 103]

A SECRET PLACE

THE WATER WAS BOILING out of the cliff face. Wild animal tracks were everywhere. My dogs were nearly chasing their tails with excitement. My five-year-old grandson would have been chasing his tail if he'd had one.

Dogs, grandson, and I were at the back of the farm in an isolated, rocky hollow. The sides are so steep the trees can hardly hold on. Nobody goes there because it's so hard to get to. Deer, coyote, turkeys, and other animals know that, and they congregate there in force.

The hollow isn't worth any money, but it's one of my favorite places in the world. It used to belong to my grandfather, then my father, now me. None of us ever did anything to harm it. I'm looking for someone who feels for it like I do, and will protect it in the future. I hope it's my grandson.

As the head of the hollow is a huge spring, forming a stream that would be called a river in some parts of the world. The trees are so big they meet over the top of the creek, almost like a tunnel. The creek is very swift and very cold, running over many little waterfalls and rapids with a solid rock bottom.

There are many steep, deep side hollows with their own springs and creeks running into the main hollow. It seems like the hollows are made up of many and very different little climates. The kinds of trees and wildflowers and ferns and moss and mushrooms are constantly changing.

The Indians liked the place, too. They left more evidence of being there than the white man has, unbelievable as that sounds. When I was a kid in the early '30s, the local moonshiners would meet there every fourth of July. After squirrel hunting on the way, they would gather at the spring, eat squirrel, sample plenty of each other's moonshine, tell lies and brag on their dogs and guns.

When I was there with my grandson, a state forester had entered the hollow in a two-state conservation contest. The judges were due later in the week. On that day my grandson walked through a mudhole that already had deer and turkey tracks in it. By chance, the judges saw the mudhole. The hollow won the contest, and I think that mudhole was a big part of it.

But on this day there was no one there but my grandson, my dogs and me. Being an old man, I sat and watched and listened to that magic spring and thought old man thoughts. Eternal spring, eternal life, eternity in general. My grandson and dogs, being much smarter, just ran around in circles, investigating things. They would all return to me, and in their different ways tell me what they had seen, or thought they had seen, or wished they had seen.

When we were ready to go, my grandson wanted to know who knew about that place. Especially he wanted to know if his older sister knew about it. I told him no. He said, "Good. Let's let this be our secret place, okay?"

Pvt. Robert Thrasher

Billy Bradford (1945) – Army buddy

Fred Ablin (1945) – Army buddy from Chicago

Bob Thrasher, Billy Bradford from Texas, Irving Warnasch
from Orange, N.J. (1945)

Fred Ablin and Warren McCoy – Germany, 1945

Photo of Robert, his parents and siblings around 1941

Robert at age 10

Robert with pet hen, siblings Jo Ann and Paul

Robert's wife, Bessie, around 1947

Engineers Work Fast to Bridge Erft

Soldier-artist Robert S. Robison sketched this view of the Erft Canal Bridge erected by 99th Inf. Div. engineers

99th Doggies Smash Way To Dig in On Rhine Banks

By Robert S. Robison
Stars and Stripes Unit Correspondent

WITH 99th DIV.—The Third Armd. had laid a bridge across the Erft Canal before Bergheim, whose ancient city gates guard the highway to Cologne, but when tanks ran into trouble from the high, wooded Hill 140 on their left, 395th Regt. doggies stormed the town .

In a sweeping and bloody maneuver up the hill, and through a miniature Argonne forest of dug-in Jerries, they seized the high ground and the tanks rolled on to Cologne as the 395th hung the usual placard over the city gates.

By this time, the rest of the division was crossing the Erft in several places further up. While the 395th held the flank, the 394th fought through and around them and the 393rd on the left, raced toward the Rhine.

The Engineers moved into Bedburg and finished two bridges in less than 12 hours, and as the heavy stuff came over, the left flank moved as fast as the doughfeet could walk and sent back the prisoners. Then the 394th ran into trouble in the fortified towns, things began to get rough.

Task Force Luters, reinforced by tanks, T.D.s and infantry roared into Deikum, to the River's bank as foot soldiers of the 393rd came close on their heels. -

As the 394th worked forward in the center, the Nazis began to ferry stuff across the river, but the big guns of the 3. nd Artillery caught barges containing what was left of a division Hq and blew them to smithereens in mid-river.

The advance was so fast the doggies caught a kitchen train in the hill above Neurath and it still sits there, the stove hitched to its wagon, and carrot soup all over the road. A platoon of the Engineers A Co. barged into a factory office and heard the phone ringing. Answering it, they found it was the home office in Dusseldorf calling to see where the Americans were.

Four Jerries were caught with their glasses down as GIs interrupted a private party.

Co. K of the 393rd dug in on the Rhine and sent the CG, Maj. Gen. Walter E. Lauer of Brooklyn NY a bottle of water from the river.

and several hundred freed English, Russian and French PWs who had been forced laborers a few hours previously

The Checkerboard men claim they were the first infantry division in the First Army to reach the Rhine. .

FROM

TO: **MRS B. H. THRASHER**
BLOOMINGTON,
INDIANA
R.R.5

Pfc. Robert W. Thrasher   35076126

Co. L, 395th INF APO 449

%o P.M. New York, N.Y.

[CENSOR'S STAMP]

SEE INSTRUCTION NO. 2

(Sender's complete address above)

Dear Folks,   Sat. Dec. 16, 1944
                                                                    8:00 P.M.

Received a letter from you written Dec. 4 day before yesterday but still no Xmas packages, altho some of the other boys have started getting theirs. Well, I have what should be pleasent news to you(pleasant in that it's no worse), I'm in a hospital with pneumonia. Got here yesterday but expect to go back to the front in a short time as they tell me they have it cleared up soon. I feel O.K. and lucky that I'm here in this condition after seeing the condition some of the boys are in. Things are getting pretty rough around this neck of the woods now and even before I left our squad had been hit pretty hard. I feel almost like a shirker being back here with only pneumonia but it was getting to the place where I wasn't much good to them up there. Guess I won't get any mail as long as I'm here so that will be an incentive to get well faster. Things are really nice back here - plenty to eat, lots of sleep, no night patrals, no nothing; just lay around and read and sleep all day. Well, had better quit for now.
                                                        Love, Robert

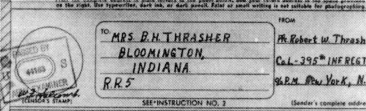

TO: MRS. B.H. THRASHER
BLOOMINGTON,
INDIANA
R.R.5

SEE·INSTRUCTION NO. 2

FROM
Pk. Robert W. Thrasher 35076106
Co.L-395ᵗʰ INF REGT. A.P.O.449
%.P.M. New York, N.Y.

(Sender's complete address above)

Dear Folks:

Germany
Jan. 2, 1945

Thought I'd let you know I'm still kicking. Have been out of the hospital since the day before X-mas, but only started getting my packages yesterday, I got six. Sorry I haven't written sooner, but because of the cold and various other reasons haven't written sooner. Things have been pretty hot around here lately. Yesterday morning just after sunrise about 50 German planes came over us at tree-top level. We could see the pilots sitting in them and the bombs under the wings, but they didn't bother us although I know they seen us. Our ack-ack knocked down several of them the. Have seen a few good dog-fights here lately, too. If the setting had been different this morning would have been one of the most beautiful sunrises I ever seen. I raised up out of my foxhole, half froze, and the sun was just coming up, there is snow on the ground and frost on all the trees and fences, it was shining and the clouds were all changing color. Some scene, but you had to remember that the Germans were just across the valley looking right back at you. Every nite is like the Fourth of July, buzz bombs, artillery and mortars, flares, and tracers flying around all night. Sure will be glad to see summer come, won't be froze all the time at least. Got a little bit of everything in my packages, and I can use everything I got, have already made a big start on the chocolates. Had put Mollie's boat on a string and am wearing it around my neck, have read too many fiction books, I guess. Well, have about run out of anything to say.

Love,
Robert
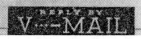

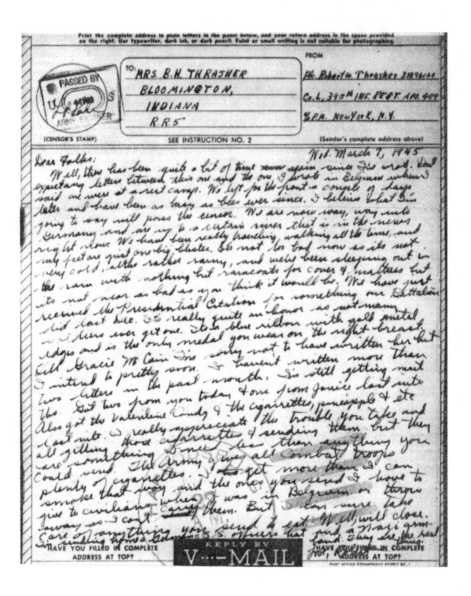

TO: MRS. B.N. THRASHER
BLOOMINGTON,
INDIANA
R.R.5

FROM
Pfc. Robert N. Thrasher 35896011
Co. L, 39th INF. REGT. A.M. 408
% P.M. New York, N.Y.

(CENSOR'S STAMP)   SEE INSTRUCTION NO. 2   (Sender's complete address above)

Wed. March 7, 1945

Dear Folks;

Well, there has been quite a lot of time some again since I've wrote. Kept expecting letters between this and and the one I wrote in Belgium when I said we were at a rest camp. We left for the front a couple of days later and have been as busy as bees ever since. I believe that this is going to very well pass the censor. We are now way, way into Germany and on my to a certain sector that is in the news right now. We have been really traveling, walking all the time, and only feet are mud on big blister. It's not so bad now as it's not very cold, little rather rainy, and we've been sleeping out in the rain with nothing but raincoats for cover & mattress but it's not near as bad as you think it would be. We have just received the Presidential Citation for something our Battalion did last bbe. It really quite an honor as not many soldiers ever get one. It's a blue ribbon with gold pieted edges and is the only medal you wear on the right breast. Got Gracie McCain Sis why not to have written her but I intend to pretty soon. I haven't written more than two letters in the past month. Sis still getting mail the. Got two from you today & one from Janice last nite. Also got the Valentine Candy & the cigarettes, pineapple & etc & cut out. I really appreciate the trouble you take and all getting those cigarettes & sending them but they were something sweet. Say than anything you could send. The army gives all combat troops plenty cigarettes. get more than I can smoke that way and the ones you send I have to give to civilians where I was in Belgium or throw away as I can't carry them. But they were late. Care anything before. Well will close.

Phrosh

HEADQUARTERS 99TH INFANTRY DIVISION
APO 449
United States Army

GENERAL ORDER)

NUMBER   16)   6 March 1945

BATTLE HONORS--THIRD BATTALION THREE NINETY FIFTH INFANTRY

Under the provisions of Section IV, War Department Circular 333 (1943) and
Section VII, Circular 2, Headquarters First United States Army, dated 4 January
1945, citation of the following unit, as approved by the Commanding General, First
United States Army, is announced. The citation reads as follows:

The Third Battalion, Three Ninety Fifth Infantry Regiment, is cited for
outstanding performance of duty in action against the enemy during the period
16 to 19 December 1944, near Hofen, Germany. During the German offensive in
the Ardennes, the Third Battalion, Three Ninety Fifth Infantry Regiment was
assigned the mission of holding the Monschau - Eupen - Liege Road. For four
successive days the battalion held this sector against combined German tank
and infantry attacks, launched with fanatical determination and supported by
heavy artillery. No reserves were available to the battalion, and the situation
was desperate. Disregarding personal safety and without rest the men fought
vigorously to hold their positions against hostile penetrations. On at least
six different occasions the battalion was forced to place artillery concentra-
tions dangerously close to its own positions in order to repulse penetrations
and restore its lines. On other occasions, men came out of their fixed defenses
and engaged in desperate hand-to-hand fighting in order to repel enemy assault
teams. The enemy artillery was so intense that communications were generally
out. The men carried out missions without orders when their positions were
penetrated or infiltrated. They killed Germans coming at them from the front,
flanks, and rear. Outnumbered five to one, they inflicted casualties in the
ratio of eighteen to one. With ammunition supplies dwindling rapidly, the men
obtained German weapons and utilized ammunition obtained from casualties to
drive off the persistent foe. Despite fatigue, constant enemy shelling, and
ever-increasing enemy pressure, the Third Battalion, Three Ninety Fifth Infantry
Regiment prevented the German break-through from extending to the Monschau area,
guarded a 6,000 yard front, and destroyed seventy-five percent of three German
Infantry regiments. The courage and devotion to duty displayed by members of
the Third Battalion, Three Ninety Fifth Infantry Regiment, in the face of
overwhelming odds was in keeping with the highest traditions of the military
service.

The Third Battalion, Three Ninety Fifth Infantry Regiment, is entitled to the
citation streamer. The individuals assigned or attached to this unit on the
occasion for which citation was awarded are entitled to wear the Distinguished Unit
Badge. Individuals subsequently assigned or attached are entitled to wear the
Distinguished Unit Badge only so long as they remain with the unit.

R E S T R I C T E D

General Order #16, Div Hq, 99th Inf Div, 6 Mar 45, continued.

By command of Major General LAUER:

R. B. WARREN,
Lt Col, GSC,
Chief of Staff.

OFFICIAL:

JOHN R. ACHOR,
Lt Col, AGD,
Adjutant General.

DISTRIBUTION:

TAG, Decorations & Awards Branch
   Munitions Bldg, Washington 25, D. C.. 3
CG, European Theater of Operations,
   Attn: G-1.............................. 3
CG, 12th Army Gp, Attn: 37th MRU......... 2
CG, 1st US Army, Attn: G-1 Misc.......... 1
CG, VII Corps............................ 1
CG, V Corps.............................. 1
Historian, 99th Inf Div.................. 5
AG, D & A Sec............................10

Plus Distribution "D"
Plus 1000 copies to 3d Bn, 395th Inf.

Germany
Tues. April 17, 1945

Dear Folks:

It's a nice warm day here today, and has been for past few days. I got two letters from you today and one from Gracie the other day. I also got a little package of caramels last nite, the two big packages came the other nite, at a rather bad time. We were just leaving for a town. I managed to carry them altho some of the boys threw theirs away without even opening them. We ate one box and the chocolates out of another, then we had to go guard some PWs, and when we came back someone – curious GI's, or someone had made off with both boxes of cookies. Maybe they were hungrier than I was tho. The other day we took a town that had over twenty three thousand allied prisoners in it, mostly Russian. Everyone but the Russians were in pretty fair shape, but as Russia doesn't belong to the Red Cross the Russians got only what the Germans fed them, and that is almost nothing. Some of the prisoners had been there for five years and were crazy, young men of twenty five looked sixty. Some of them were so happy to see us, they cried, others just

83

shook your hand and wanted to kiss you. They There were so many of them and they were so hungry we had to guard them and keep them in the prison or else they'd have run all over the country jamming road, killing civilians and etc. It was quite an experience. We didn't have any food for so many but they have been fed now. We found some of them who had stepped out and dug up a dead horse and were fighting over it. One was eating on the tail with the hair still on it. They were eating out of garbage cans and worse. Believe it or not. They were dying at the rate of over a hundred a day. 150 died the day we took the town. Things have quieted down here now but we'll move to a not so quiet sector. The other day when we were spearheading on tanks we caught the krauts with their pants down. We must have taken five thousands prisoners and untold amounts of equipment. We overran their columns retreating along the roads — mostly horses and wagons which couldn't outrun tanks. There were dead and wounded horses and men in both ditches along the road. Not a pleasant site — but better than Americans lying there. In one truck I found the payroll and have one socket full of marks — fifteen hundred of them. They are good in unoccupied Germany and even good in this town but they don't have anything much to buy. I now have two .35 cal. pistols, one on each hip. I feel like Tim McCoy or someone. Oh yes, I also got a package from Ada the other day—had home-made cookies, candy bars, gum, & a fruit cake in it. Hope their war ends soon and they don't send us to the Pacific—that would really be hell. Well, have about run down. Got the three picture the other day.

Love,
Robert

August Ullrich · Elfershausen (Mainfr.)

TIEF- UND STRASSENBAU · WALZENBETRIEB

Wasserversorgungs- und Kanalisationsanlagen · Erd-, Beton-, Eisenbetonarbeiten · Ausführung von
Walzarbeiten · Pflasterungen · Teer-, Asphalt-, Einstreu- und Tränkdecken, Oberflächenbehandlung

Fernsprecher · Bernsdorf 822
Bankkonten:
Bayerische Staatsbank, Würzburg
Kreissparkasse Hammelburg
Postscheck-Konto · Nürnberg Nr. 20756

Ihre Zeichen   Mein Zeichen   Ihre Nachricht vom   ELFERSHAUSEN,

Obrehausen, Germany
Tues June 19, 1945

Dear Folks:

Didn't hear from you today but have heard from you pretty regular here lately. I still don't know anything definite as to what time I'll be back in the states or what outfit I'll be in. But they are sending guys out of the company almost daily to divisions going to the states. I'll probably be there sometime in July at the latest. And it's definite I'll go to the Pacific, just hope I can stand that on top of this. As many men as there are in the U.S. it would seem that one guy should only have to sweat out one war. I want to stay here as long as I can because that will be one less in the Pacific. I can't think, let alone write as a bunch of the boys are batting the breeze in the room.

Next day—
Still no mail. About the school business, I'm signed up for a few interesting subjects (they don't have any interesting ones) but I doubt if I'll be here long enough to attend any classes. Yes I stopped sending the $15 home, or rather the Army stopped taking mine. Well, it's a nice hot day today, but the nights are all cold. We still stand guard from 4 to 6 hrs. every 24 hr. In combat we sometimes stood as much as 18 hrs. a nite for several nites running. Quite a change, but we don't appreciate it like we should. We also have a little calisthenics and drill every day. It's been so long since I've done any work I've enjoyed doing that I sometimes wonder what'll come of me if I ever get out of the Army. For a long time we just worked to keep from dying. Alloy we recognize it and talk about it. That guy, I wonder if I should try and go ahead to school, but maybe I'll snap out of it. I don't know if I'll get any good souvenirs for you or not. If we stop in France and I have any money I will. I seen a lot of good ones while we were fighting

but I couldn't carry them along to the end of the war because of weight, no room, and I'd probably have broken them.

Tell Paul he'd better get some ammo lined up for that new T.22, cause when I get home I'll want to shoot it. I'd also like to fish a little but I doubt if I will. We do a little fishing over here with hand grenades, we throw the grenade in the river, the dead fish come to the top and we swim in and get them. We do quite a bit of deer hunting too. We are going to have a deer barbecue Sunday nite. We for this week we've killed over ten and have them in a cold storage locker in town.

I'd hoped to do a little chasing around when I get home but if the tires are bad I'll have to hitchhike. I'll just flash my Combat Infantry Badge and should get a ride right away. Do you see many of them around town now and do people know what they mean, or do they think you get them for being a good shot with the water pistol?

Well, I should be home in July or August, not too bad a time. Have got to close now as I go on guard in a minute.

Love.
Robert

Café Marguery
34 Boulevard Bonne Nouvelle
Paris, France

Dear Folks:

I'm not exactly in the mood to write tonite but will try anyhow. It's too early to go to bed and unless I go to a movie there's not much else to do tonight that I care about. I went out to see my girl this afternoon at 1:00 PM and I didn't get back till 7:00 PM. It takes almost an hour and a half to make the round trip by subway. Got the letter with the comb today and have been getting mail pretty regular here lately. Received one over a week ago, but no package yet. But it's too soon to expect it I guess. If you have to have a request to send packages now I will request one now. I solemnly swear that receiving a package wouldn't hurt me at all. So Wyatts are all hepped up about Bob going to another stand. I feel for them all, but several of us had to do things we didn't like in this war. You don't have to let them know I said so naturally, as it wouldn't make them like it anymore.

88

Still no idea as to when I'll get home, but it'll be sometime next year, I imagine. Have you decided what you are going to get for Christmas yet. I'm glad to hear we've finally got a well. So being where it is at you could pipe water to the house and barn, couldn't you? I suppose Lloyd wondered why I didn't answer the letter he wrote me last March. I did, but found out later that I put the wrong APO on it, so I guess he never got it. As I said I'm not feeling like writing tonite and I'm having a hard time filling up space. I can't write local gossip because you don't know any one I do around these parts. I got a letter from one of the boys in my old platoon the other day, besides the one you sent from Albin. I've been wondering if you read Albin's letter. If you did you found that we don't mince words when we write to one another. I want to look up some of the boys out of the platoon after I get home as some of us were closer than brothers, I think. But I may never do it. It's too easy to forget people and things. That's what causes so much trouble in the world. I think most people have forgotten this war all ready. Not entirely, but forgotten really what it meant. Well, I'd better knock off. I just can't seem to get going. I'll have to wait till I get all excited about something.

Love
Robert

Gare d' L'Est, Paris
Jan. 7, 1946

Dear Folks:

When I started thinking back I discovered I hadn't written in a week or so, and so you won't think I'm either home or dead I'll write some now. I've not received any mail for a few days but then the mail situation is really screwed up over here now. I got the package with the cigarettes just the other. Andrée wants me to thank you and Jo Ann for the stockings and lip-stick fingernail-nail polish. She bought a couple of things for you and Jo but I haven't mailed them yet. I'll probably just bring them home with me. There are souvenirs of Paris with a thing-a-ma-jig to hold ink and lay your pen on. She got me a cigarette case for Christmas and I gave her a bracelet. I got a three day pass over Xmas and went with her and her folks to see some of their relatives who live in a little town named Ouluvouf, it's in Normandy near Cherbourg. We had a good time. They had plenty to eat and it was good. I'm learning to eat new things practically every day and like French food pretty well now. They also had plenty to drink. Christmas Eve we walked a couple of miles to another town and went to midnight mass at a Catholic church. I took several pictures but I waited until the morning we left to do it and didn't take them where I'd intended. This area was one of the little rounds of the invasion and there were 5 American tanks just outside town that had been knocked out. I think I've told you but I'm not working at Mess No 5 any more but at one of the railway stations called Gare l'Est – which means "Station of the East."

We also had some pictures taken awhile back here in Paris. They aren't too good of her altho they look like her. I'm sending two in this letter. I still don't know when I'll start home but it shouldn't be too awful long now. Since I got that letter about the tractor I've been anxious as hell to get started. I'll bet Paul and Dad are tickelled pink. Are you still going to get the new car. The only thing I've driven since I left the states has been a Kraut motorcycle, so I'll have to do a little practicing before I start again, I imagine. I see Paris all the time now as I'm in charge of the ration-truck and we go around to different warehouses to pick up rations and various other things. I know Paris practically as well as a taxi driver now. I got a letter today from Arlie — his still in Germany with a couple of the other boys from the platoon. I and the other platoon buddies are here in France guarding PW's and so forth. Hope to hear from you soon.

Love,
Robert

UNCLE JOE

DURING THE WAR, the newspapers referred to Joseph Stalin as "Uncle Joe." I was also referred to as "Uncle Joe" because I always seemed to know what was going to happen in advance and reacted accordingly. My fellow soldiers joked that I had a "hot line" to Joseph Stalin. I guess I was just psychic. A story written by one of my fellow soldiers appears in a copy of "LOVE NOTES" where I am referred to as "Uncle Joe." "LOVE NOTES" refers to Company "L" which is the name we gave to our newsletter while still in Germany after the war ended. I was also a frequent editor in addition to composing short stories and poems and a few appear in this book.

(The editors and publishers of "Love Notes" are not only proud but honored to present Mr. Joseph Thrasher a new star upon the horizon of poetry.)

POEM

When I came to the Army
back in nineteen forty-three,
I couldn't bend an elbow
or scarcely touch my knees.
(Look at me now-no knees)
I took a 3-33 shirt
and my 45-13 pants
Drug behind me in the dirt.
But after two years of hut-two,
I look damn nice in my clothes.
And by wrapping my right arm around
my left ankle,
I can hang in mid-air by my nose.
That's a slight exaggeration
I'm forced to admit.
But what the hell.
We all lie a bit.
I'll now take a ten-minute break
As I can hardly hold my pen.
These damn calisthenics are killing us
don't you think so, men?

(Three years later, between poses for
advertisements of Dr. Marvel's Body
Building Courses.)
There's no figure in all the nation
Better than mine, I'll bet you.
And you'll get more exercise than I,
By bending to tie your shoe.
Just saw the former "shape" Rembert,
Go by on the way to the clink.
He's head spike-driver on the B. & O.,
And looks like a model of a blimp-k.

This straight jacket fits real nice.
I thank you.
If you've got the guts to do this
you can get a section viii, too.

CHARACTER COLYUM
(appears in LOVE NOTES newsletter)

—⊃≻●≼⊂—

This morning we were at a loss for an interesting character to write up, until Thrasher dribbled into our room and collapsed on the bed. Robert Thrasher – belovedly called "Uncle Joe" by his buddies to whom he has put the screws many times was born on the lower ear of a cornstalk on Rural Route 5, Bloomington, Indiana. His early life was spent swinging from one row of corn to another and playfully pushing his grandmother into the well. He still remembers his little recess away from the world where he dreamed his dreams and planned the plans for the future – the outhouse. It was here, as with many of us, that his first vice was discovered and cultivated – smoking. After the evening repast of pig's knuckles and rhubarb, he would retire to the outhouse with a pack of "Lucky Cornsilks" and his matches and smoke to his little hearts delight. One night his father caught him and tried to take his cigarettes away. Mr. Thrasher was never seen again. But the moans that emitted from the outhouse during the night frightened the family for days.

Even now it is dangerous to try to bum a ciggy from him. His friends and neighbors finally decided that the army needed a man of Joe's character, so then he went, tar, feathers and all. He amazed them by making an IQ score of 16 and was therefore for AFTF. After three terms of engineering and crap-shooting, Joe was finally trapped by the board of health in the school latrine and was shipped to the 99th Division.

He was immediately made a first scout because of his sharp senses, aggressiveness and repulsive character. He made Pfc due to his industry, stamina, and something he had on his platoon Sergeant. The rest is a familiar story, a nightmare of inspections, trains, crap-games, PO(?) boats, oceans, England and finally Germany. They say that the only reason Von Rundstedt tried his break through in December was to drive Thrasher out of Germany into France, and in that way demoralize the entire rear echelon, It didn't work, though, and Germany sweated Joe out until now. Joe just sits around these days like the rest of us, counting his points on his fingers and toes. He hasn't got many, either – points, I mean. Of course, he is perfectly normal. Why shouldn't he be? He has ten fingers just like the rest of us, six on one and four on the other.

Well, here's our chance to end this little masterpiece and sneak away, so we warn one and all he's still on the loose, so be careful. You'll recognize him by his snappy gait, something like step-and fetch-it. He is really a good kid, too, if you watch him closely and don't believe a thing he says.

+ + + + + +

LOVE-NOTES

Co L, 395 Inf Regt

Vol. 1   25 June 1945   No 6

"FRATERNIZATION FROLICS" COMING SOON

During the latter part of the week, "Fraternization Frolics", a show presented by the 395th Inf. Regt. is going to run two nights at Battalion's newly decorated theatre. All "L" Co. will be able to see it.

Performances have been given at Regimental Hq. and the show is now touring the Battalions in the Regiment. It has been very enthusiastically received by all who have seen it. Memories are recalled of "Supermammy", the famous musical comedy presented back in the States. Many members of the cast are the same.

All will enjoy the performances of Frank Wagner and Murrey Arnold who handle their numerous parts most excellently.

(continued on 4)

LIBERATION

For all you battle-scarred vets of the kitchen--good news. Sgt. Larson is turning in his ate-l reinforced cat-o'-ninetails to the scrap drive because the Geneva Convention protects his new German KP's from its lashing. We also hear that Cutone is taking German Lessons. He is walking around muttering under his breath, "Waschen teller, schnell!" Puppy is wondering if any of them can get together with him on "The Rolling Blues", and Sgt. Wagner is making a shoulder holster for his carbine. Machine guns and anti-personnel mines are being dug around the store room, and every night the guards hear a slushing scraping noise til the wee hours. Is that bomb shelter finished yet, John?

+++++

"L" PLAYS HOST

Last night "L" Co. played host in what we hope will be a series of entertainments to the girls of the WAC detatchment of the 9th AF stationed in Bad Kessingen. Yes, they're real live American girls --just like the ones we left back home.

After the arrival of the girls, there was a short time alloted to making friendships...a minute or two, I think it took. Beaucoup beer and wine was on hand to make things just a bit more gay. And believe me, it did just that.

Then there was dancing in the rooms of ye old mess hall, which the girls thought was "the most adoreable place". Of course, most of us were a bit rusty with our steps, but I don't think that any girl lost more than three toes. At least, that's what their medic reported.

Following this short dance program, there was the supper for which we had been preparing for a couple of weeks. The deer which almost all the men had helped to kill, was bar-b-qued by T 5 Ed Burgess over an open pit. This, with the onions and rolls, was a taste of what we used to have back home.

After dinner, there was a real jam session in the back dining room. Of course, everyone was feeling quite well at the time, so there was quite a bit of jitterbugging and rug cutting, even if we don't have a rug.

Those who made the party possible we give our thanks; Dick Weinstein for starting the ball to rolling; Lt. Holcomb for keeping it going; "Sandy" for her publicity over at Hotel Victoria; Sgt. Larson for the dinner, and Special Service Officer of 9th AF for the use of his records.

(The editors and publishers of "Love Notes" are not only proud but honored to present Mr. Joseph Thrasher a new star upon the horizon of poetry)

POEM

When I came to the Army
back in ninteen forty-three,
I couldn't bend an elbow
or scarcely touch my knees.
(Look at me now—no knees)
I took a 3-33 shirt
and my 45-13 pants.
Drug behind me in the dirt.
But after two years of hut-two,
I look damn nice in my clothes.
And by wrapping my right arm around,
my left ankle,
I can hang in mid-air by my nose.
That's a slight exageration
I'm forced to admit.
But what the hell,
We all lie a bit.
I'll now take a ten-minute break
As i can hardly hold my pen.
These damn calisthentics are killing us
Don't you think so, men?
(Three years later, between poses for
advertisements of Dr. Marvel's Body
Building Course.)
There's no figure in all the nation
Better thanmine, I'll bet you.
And you'll get more exercise than I,
By bending to tie your shoe.
Just saw the former "Shape" Rembert,
Go by on the way to the clink.
He's head spike-driver on the B.& O.,
And looks like a model of a blimp-k.

ANNOUNCEMENT
Save your bitches for next week's new "Love Note's" column, "The Bitching Well! Please submit all bitches to this office in writting.

(V-Packet Continued)

J. P. O'Donnell would like to have it announced that for a short time only his Silver Star will be on display at 1st Platoon CP- at reasonable price, of course.

Dusenberry says that last weeks pin-up looks a hell of a lot like Bonnie Lou Smoot —what a gal!

C-More "Hersney Bars" Motin made a big hit with all the WACS in Bad Kissingen the other night. Of course all he could say was "Ugh" when they asked where hehad served his three years overseas.

All the boys, after seeing Satan Bloom in the character of "Bed Room Pin-up" are trying to make appointments for"sleefen".

(Continued from Page 5)
McKeown and Tanner scored for the second platoon while Grubb, Thate, Kuhn and Runge scored for the third.

This straight jacket fits real nice, I think you.
If you've got the guts to do this You can get a Section VIII, too.

CHARACTER COLYUM

This morning we were at a loss for an interesting character to write up, until Thrasher dribbled into our room and collapsed on the bed. Robert Thrasher--belovedly called "Uncle Joe" by his buddies to whom he has put the screws many times--was born on the lower ear of a cornstalk on Rural Route 5, Bloomington Indiana. His early life was spent swinging from one row of corn to another and playfully pushing his grandmother into the well. He still remembers his little recess away from the world where he dreamed his dreams and planned his plans for the future-- the outhouse. It was here, as with many of us, that his first vice was discovered and cultivated-- smoking. After the evening repast of pig's knuckles and rhubarb, he would retire to the outhouse with a pack of "Lucky Cornsilk" and his matches and smoke to his little hearts delight. One night his father caught him and tried to take his cigarettes away. Mr. Thrasher was never seen again. But the moans that emitted from the outhouse during the night frightened the family for days.

Even now it is dangerous to try to bum a ciggy from him. His friends and neighbors finally decided that the army needed a man of Joe's character, so then he went, war, feathers, and all. He amazed them by making an IQ score of 16 and was therefore eligible for ASTP. After three terms of engineering and cigar-shooting, Joe was finally trapped by the board of health in the school latrine and was shipped to the 99th Division. He was immediately made a first scout because of his sharp senses, aggressiveness, and repulsive character. He made Pfc due to his industry, stamina, and something he had on his platoon sergeant. The rest is a familiar story, a nightmare of inspection, trains, crap-games, PO's, boats, oceans, England, and finally Germany. They say that the only reason Von Runstedt tried his breakthrough in December was to drive Thrasher out
(Continued on page 4)

In case you aren't doing anything next Wednesday afternoon, drop down to the old swimming hole. If you are doing something, drop it and come down anyway. The WACs are coming back for a repeat performance. This time it is for a swim. If you intend to swim, be sure to bring a suit of some description, for this is strictly one of those affairs at which suits are a must. For those who think there is one of the girls who actually cares, this is quite a chance to solidify relations. And for the ones who didn't get along so well, this is another chance. Some one; come all!

rary Editor--
        Capt. Erskine B. Wickersham
Editor--Pfc. Billy Bradford
Adviser--1st Sgt. James J. Turley
Circulation Manager--Sgt. John Kembert
Reporters--Pfc. Irving R F Wernsuch,
Pfc. Richard Weinstein, Pfc. Paul
Buhl, Pfc. J. E. O'Donnell, Pfc. Fred
Ablin

V
PACKET

Who told us that Sgt. Jake's dancing just wouldn't quit last night? It couldn't have been that cute little WAC who limped home muttering something about her luck.

++++++

Three of the boys got their faces slapped last night when they forgot themselves and asked three WACs to "promimaden in wald". Or did they forget themselves?

++++++

Sgt. Scott made his yearly visit to Co. last night, to see the boys, of course, and upon arrival was immediately surrounded by scores of GI's pleading "tell me about the points, will ya, Scotty. Tell me, will ya, huh?

++++++

Welcome home to Sgts. Vrzak, Duszynski, and Bruner and all the other boys. Don't take your shoes off at night, men, we'll all be going together.

++++++

What did I ever do to deserve this, cried 3 Sgt. Nate Thompson over a glass of beer. "All I ever ask them to do is to get up for reveille, and they just lie there and stare at me; they're always staring. I'm not being mean, am I? I just can't stand it any longer!"

++++++

Why is it that every time a groovy number appears on the loud speaker, you will always hear an Australian sound off? Personally we think that Joe Mysliewiec is a better husky mover than musician, especially after eleven o'clock at night.

+++ ++

Sgt. Sammara tells us that he saw the WACs were picking flowers in the back yard last night, but the way the blankets disappeared off the clothes line we would say different.

JOKES OF THE WEEK

Sir Charles came home from a very long trip and went up to the best bedroom where he found Sir James in bed with Lady Charl.. He was very indignant and said, "How could you do this, Lady Charles. You, a descendent of the Queen, your mother was Lady in Waiting, and I from the line of Sir Walter Raleigh. And you, Sir James, you could at least stop awhile I am talking.

++++ +

Liza, surrounded by her brood of 12, got a good laugh out of the proposition by the old maid social-welfare worker. "No, ma'm, thank you," she chuckled. "Ah wouldn't be interested in no birth control. It might be all right fo' ladies like you'all, ma'm, but Ah's married and don' need it."

++++++

THIS SPACE

COMPLIMENTS OF

PX MODERN--   Bradford-Ablin

(Character Colyum Continued)

of Germany into France, and in this way demoralize the entire rear echilon. It didn't work, though, and Germany sweated Joe out until now. Joe just sits around these days, like the rest of us, counting his points on his fingers and toes. He hasn't got many, either--points, I mean. Of course, he is perfectly normal. Why shouldn't he be? He has ten fingers just like the rest of us, six on one hand and four on the other.

Well, here's our chance to end this little masterpiece and sneak away, so we warn one and all he's still on the loose, so be careful. You'll recognize him by his snappy gait, something like Step-and-Fetch-It. He is really a good kid, tho, if you watch him closely and don't believe a thing he says.

++++++

Congratulations are in order for Robert "Pete" Peterson of the first pl... ... ... yesterday, and although he is too modest to admit it, we think he is perfect material for the CBI.

++++ +

Roster as of May, 1944 Cp Maxey
Company "L" 395th First Lt. Sy Saffer
3rd Platoon

Plt Sgt. Billups
Sgt. Pyatt
Pfc Wilkenson   Runner
Pfc Sykes   Runner

1st

Sgt Taylor	Sq Ldr
Pfc Runge	1st Sct
Pfc Tromble	2nd Sct
Pfc Oxford	Bar
Pfc Wadley	Ass.
Pvt Toy	Amo Br
Pfc Bradford	Rifleman
Pfc Snodgrass	Rifleman
Pfc Biesboer	Rifleman
Pfc Belcher	Rifleman
Pfc Zarnfoller	Rifleman
Sgt Mitchell	Ass. Ldr.

2nd

S/Sgt Murray	Sq Ldr
Pfc Thrasher	1st Sct
Pfc Sopchak	2nd Sct
Pfc Furno	Bar
Pfc Butler	Ass.
Pvt Warnasch	Amo Br
Pfc Kuhn	Rifleman
Pfc Vietri	Rifleman
Pvt Vizzini	Rifleman
Pvt Ablin	Rifleman
Pvt Skolba	Rifleman
Sgt Wall	Ass. Ldr.

3rd

Sgt Olimpi	Sq. Ldr.
Pfc Fitzgerald	1st Sct
Pfc Finklea	2nd Sct
Pfc Olson	Bar
Pvc Regal	Asst
Pfc Walter	Amo Br
Pvt Hartman	Rifleman
Pvt Wienstein	Rifleman
Pvt Duesenberry	Rifleman
Pvt Bossham	Rifleman
Pvt Theve	Rifleman
Sgt Siemers	Ass Ldr

About The Author

Robert Wyatt Thrasher served in WWII. Over the past twenty years, he has been recording his "memories," as he prefers to call them, of his war experiences. Some of these stories have appeared in the Army Newspaper "Checkerboard - 99th Infantry." He has also written short stories about his childhood of growing up in Harrodsburg, Indiana.

Robert is retired from the US Post Office. He and Bessie are the parents of six children and continue to live on their Popcorn Road farm west of Harrodsburg.

Robert, at age 80, with Great-grandson Austin

Printed in the United States
127846LV00005B/1-18/A